ESSENCE OF DHARMA, YOGA & SPIRITUALITY

ESSENCE OF DHARMA, YOGA & SPIRITUALITY

RADHA KRISHNA KUMAR

Published by Zorba Books, February 2023
Website: www.zorbabooks.com
Email: info@zorbabooks.com

Title: **Essence of Dharma, Yoga & Spirituality**
Author Name: Radha Krishna Kumar

Printbook ISBN :- 978-93-95217-23-1
Ebook ISBN :- 978-93-95217-25-5

Zorba Books Pvt. Ltd. (opc)
Sushant Arcade,
Next to Courtyard Marriot,
Sushant Lok 1, Gurgaon – 122009, India

Printed in India

CONTENTS

Introduction– Life Philosophy VII

First Chapter - Religion / Sect / Creed **XI**

1. Origin of Faith And Creed 1
2. Rise of Buddhism 11
3. Jainism 25
4. Sikhism 29
5. Judaism 32
6. Christianity 35
7. Islam Religion 37
8. Rise of Sufism 40
9. The True Meaning of Dharma and its Characteristics 45

Second Chapter - Yoga **53**

10. Origin of Yoga 55
11. Jnana (Gyan) Yoga 62
12. Bhakti (Devotion) Yoga 69
13. Karma Yoga 80
14. Raja Yoga 86
15. Vipassana meditation 89

Third Chapter - Spirituality **95**

16. Spirituality 97
17. Realization of God and Soul (Consciousness) 108
18. Law of Karma 117
19. The Reality of The Principle of Rebirth 124
20. Divine Knowledge to King Parikshita 133
21. Importance of Guru 139

22. Ignorance is the Bondage of Life 144
23. Causes of Human Suffering 152
24. How to Purify the Mind? 160

Fourth Chapter - Spiritual Stories **169**

1. The Reality of Human Life 171
2. As You Sow, So You Reap 173
3. Fruit of Pious Deed and Devotion 177
4. Your God is Inside You 179
5. Thinking Makes and Ruins a Man 182
6. Pregnant Deer and Hunter 184
7. Two Monks - A Zen Story 185
8. Dirty Clothes - Zen's Tale 186
9. The Effect of Snake's Leniency 187
10. Story of Three Hermits 189
11. Value of Life 191
12. Everything Is Impermanent in This World 193
13. Result of Negative and Positive Thoughts 195
14. Both Happiness and Sorrow are Temporary 197
15. Saint Thiruvalluvar 199
16. Saint Milarepa 201
17. Story of Siddha Yogi Bodhidharma 204
18. Realisation of God 207

About the Author 209

INTRODUCTION
LIFE PHILOSOPHY

Om Shri Parameshwaraya Namah

There are many misconceptions and superstitions about the religion in this world. The communal and religious conflicts between the people of different faiths have become common phenomena. There have been many crusades in the world in the past, in which millions of people lost their lives. Therefore, it is very important to understand the basic nature of religion so that misconceptions can be removed. Right knowledge is impossible without understanding Dharma, Yoga and Spirituality.

In fact, I was reading and contemplating about these subjects for many years and during this time I got an opportunity to read the history of religion and the texts of many religions. I wanted to understand that what is the purpose of religion after all? Why is there so much controversy and conflict in the world regarding religion? The aim of religion should be to spread knowledge, nonviolence, compassion, love and happiness and not to create ignorance, hatred, division and violence. If religion is pushing the mankind into the darkness of ignorance by creating irrational and unscientific thinking, then it is not worthy of holding. "Dharayati iti dharmaah" means, that which is worth imbibing is dharma. The path of religion is that which leads to the welfare of human beings, removes the darkness of ignorance and spreads non-violence, love and compassion for all living beings so that all live in peace and harmony on this earth.

Man has been going like a herd of sheep without thinking since centuries. Whereas the sages, seer and yogis of India tried time and again to bring the people out of the darkness of ignorance through spirituality and yoga. A pure stream of knowledge is flowing through the words of Upanishads, Bhagavad Gita, Lord Buddha, Lord Mahavira, Maharishi Patanjali and Saint Kabir. We need to read and understand those to drive away our ignorance.

My purpose of writing this book is to bring human beings out of the darkness of ignorance and to create positive thinking by removing negative thoughts from human mind. Today, it is necessary that in place of violence, anger, selfishness and jealousy, the feeling of friendliness, kindness, generosity and gratitude should be manifested so that there may be happiness and love throughout world. Ignorance creates a feeling of hatred which makes the life of a man miserable.

Today the unrest is increasing in the world. Although human beings have more material comforts than before, yet man's mind is more disturbed today. If the mind is disturbed, from where will happiness be attained? Happiness is a spiritual feeling. It has nothing to do with sense pleasure.

The sages and seers of ancient times have shown us the way to live life happily and peacefully. They told that only by following the path of spirituality, yoga and meditation, we will get happiness and peace. Spirituality creates a comprehensive view of life to know - who are we after all, where have we come from and where do we go in the end? What is the nature of God? Is God corporeal or formless? Is God away from us or inside us? How will God be realized?

The path of yoga i.e., good conduct, virtue, good deed and meditation are essential for spiritual journey and awakening. This topic is discussed further in this book. An attempt has been made to write this book keeping in mind the darkness of falsehood and hypocrisy prevailing all around world. This should be removed and the light of truth and knowledge should spread. "Om, Asatoma sadgamaya, Tamasoma jyotirgamaya, Mrtyorma amritam gamaya, Om Shanti, Shanti, Shanti." (Oh Lord! lead us from the falsehood to the truth, lead us from darkness (ignorance) to light (wisdom), lead us to get out of fear of death by reminding us about the immortality of soul, Om Peace, Peace, Peace.)- (Brihadaranyaka Upanishad)

I hope that this book will contribute in your spiritual journey. It is my endeavour that the human weaknesses such as lust, anger, ego, attachment, hatred and violence should be removed from this world and the spiritual knowledge, friendliness, compassion, peace, non-violence and the spirit of universal brotherhood should be spread.

In the end, I pray to Lord to keep his grace on me. I pay obeisance to the great saints and to my departed revered parents (Mrs. Jayapati Devi & Shri Tapeshwar Kuwar) and pay thanks to my wife Mrs. Kalawati Singh. I pray to God for everyone's wellbeing.

Radha Krishna Kumar
Basant Panchami, 2022

FIRST CHAPTER -
RELIGION / SECT / CREED

1
ORIGIN OF FAITH AND CREED

The information about the pre-historic period is still very limited and hazy. The civilizations of ancient Assyria, Egypt, Greece, Mohenjo-Daro-Harappa and China are approximately about three thousand years before Christ. The history of the gradual development of human civilization is available since ten thousand years, which had come down through the Stone, Copper, Bronze and Iron Age to the river valley civilizations and from there the beginning of the historical period begins.

However, the history of the journey from monkey to man is millions of years old. Based on Charles Darwin's research and the information from other sources, it can be said that the journey of human beings from vagabond life to permanent settled life is much antique. Therefore, the history of human civilization is also very old.

Primitive human used to live nomadic life. They lived in and around the forest. They used to eat the fruits of the forests, barks and roots of shrubs and plants, flesh of animals and drank the water of rivers and streams. To protect themselves from rain, thunderstorms and storms, they used to hide in the mountain's caves where they also had to face wild ferocious animals, such as lions, tigers, cheetahs and bears. Human being's early life was very painful, struggling and risky. They always had to be vigilant. On the one side, there was natural calamity and on the other side fear of wild animals.

In the early days many people used to die due to natural calamities like landslides, volcanoes, floods, tsunamis, infectious diseases, storms and thunderstorms. The life of a primitive human being was completely dependent on the nature. So, the people loved nature but were also afraid of the natural disasters. The primitive human beings considered the nature as their protector and destroyer. This mixed form of love and fear of nature gave rise to faith and primitive people started worshiping nature for their protection.

Primitive human beings worshiped the earth, rivers, mountains, trees, sun, moon, rain, air, fire and planets and considered natural events as divine indicator. Scientific and spiritual thinking was not developed at that time, due to which man did not understand natural phenomena properly. Spiritual and philosophical thinking started about five thousand years back from today. With the rise of civilizations in the river valley, man began to live permanently in one place and his life became more stable, peaceful and gradually understanding began to develop in him. As man's economic development started, his life became more peaceful and he started understanding the secrets of nature better. Around 3500 years before Christ, Egyptian civilization in the Valley of Nile River, Mohenjo-Daro - Harappa civilization in the Valley of Indus River and Mesopotamia (Iraq) civilization developed in the valley of Tigris-Euphrates. Similarly, the civilizations of Assyria, Greece and China also developed in the valleys of rivers.

A detailed study of all the aforesaid civilizations shows that at that time in the entire world people used to worship nature along with many gods and goddesses. There was also practice of sacrifice of animals to satisfy some gods. The people of ancient Egypt followed the polytheistic religion and did idol worship like Hindus, but at that time some people also believed in the concept of monotheism. The people of ancient Egypt worshiped the sun, the moon, the Nile, the earth, the mountains, the sky, and the air. Worship of Sun and Nile was paramount. Raw (Sun God), Osiris (Death God), Thoth (Moon God), Horus etc. were the names of the important deities.

The people of ancient Mesopotamia also worshiped many deities. Similarly, many Gods and goddesses were worshiped in Greece as well. In this, Zeus (King of gods) Dionysus, Apollo, Eros, Isis,

Hermes, Hades, Chromes, Hephaestus, Posey, etc. were the major deities. The people of ancient Greece used to play in honour of the God of Olympics. This tradition was the beginning of the Olympic game. Many ancient legends and myths are described in the ancient civilization of Greece, which looks like Indian mythology and legends. There are lot of similarities between India's Hindu mythology and Greek mythology. The character is similar but the names are different in the mythology of both ancient India and ancient Greek, as for example, similarity between Indra and Zeus. Indra and Zeus, both were the kings of devas and both were having similar weapon and character. The interesting similarity is that Indra was living on Sumeru Mountain while Zeus was living at Olympus Mountain. Similarity is also seen in the case of Lanka and Trojan War. The battle against Lanka was fought after the kidnaping of queen Sita by demon king Ravana while Shri Rama was in exile, whereas Trojan War took place after the kidnapping of Queen Helen by Paris, the prince of Trojan. There is also similarity between supreme trinities, i.e., Brahma, Lord Vishnu and Lord Shiva and trinities such as Zeus, Hades and Poseidon of Greek mythology. There are also similarities between Yamadeva and Hades, Saptarishies and seven Sisters, Narada and Hermes, Daedalus and Jatayu, Sampati and Icarus, Karna of Mahabharata and Achilles, Kamadeva and Cupid.

Even today, the oldest historical and archaeological heritage of the world, such as the archaeological site of Petra in Jordan, west Asia, which is protected by UNESCO as a World Heritage is a reminder of ancient human civilization. Similarly, the pyramid of Egypt helps us to know about the ancient life of human beings. Thus, it is known fact that in the ancient times people all over the world used to worship nature as well as many gods and goddesses but in West Asia with the origin of Abrahamic religion in Jerusalem, the old worship system came to an end. It is known that Prophet Abraham who is considered the first prophet of Judaism, Christianity and Islam religion was born in Mesopotamia (Iraq) around 1500 B.C.

Many Gods and Goddesses have been worshiped along with

nature since the Vedic era in India. The principal deities of the Vedic era were Suryadeva (sun God), Pawan deva (air God), Varuna (ocean God), Aditi, Yama, Soma, Usha, Saraswathi, Mitra, Prithvi and Rudra besides king of devas, Indra. Thus, since the Vedic era, polytheism was prevalent.

The concept of monotheism was developed by the Upanishads and there is clear mention in the Upanishads regarding the nature of God. The Upanishads have described God as formless and unborn and described that God cannot be seen from senses, but it can only be realized in the deep meditation. Brahma, Atman (soul), samsara, Maya and Avidya (Ignorance) are widely mentioned in the Upanishads.

During Vedic period, rituals and yagnas were prominent. Yagnas were performed to please devas of Vedic period, in which animals were also sacrificed. In Ashvamedha Yagna the horses were sacrificed. Thus, Yajna and rituals were widely practiced in the Vedic era, but even at that time, the sages of the Upanishads called the Yajna and rituals as Avidya(ignorance) and they emphasized on the path of jnana (Knowledge). The sages of the Upanishads said that supreme goal of human life is salvation which can only be attained through the path of knowledge and for this one has to control his mind and senses. The meditation, knowledge of Brahman and soul can liberate a man from cycle of birth and death.

It is said in the Upanishads that the entire universe is cosmic, that is, God is omnipresent. The particle of God is within every human being which is called Atman (soul or consciousness). The Upanishads said that God is the truth and this world is Maya, (illusion). The sages of the Upanishads said that "Ekam Brahm, dvitiya naste neh na naste kinchan" means there is only one God but due to Maya (illusion) a person is not able to feel God. But the knowledge of Upanishads was not adopted by the wider section of Hindu society and the people kept on worshiping various deities, involved in rituals and superstitions.

In short, the entire Hindu philosophy can be broadly divided into two parts namely, Vidya and Avidya (Knowledge & Ignorance). Apart from Vedanta philosophy i.e., Upanishads, Maharishi Kapil's Samkhya philosophy and Gautama Rishi's Nyaya philosophy are the treasure of knowledge. Maharishi Kanad's Vaisheshika philosophy which says that the smallest, indivisible, indestructible part of the world is an atom (anu). All physical things such as the earth, water, fire and air are a combination of atoms. Maharishi Patanjali's yoga philosophy teaches the human beings to seek knowledge and remove ignorance in order to get moksha, liberation but on the other hand, the priestly rituals which were widespread in Hinduism were leading the human beings to ignorance. Vedanta philosophy has repeatedly emphasized that avidya is the root cause of bondage and a person who is ignorant can never attain liberation. That is, only after removal of ignorance, anyone can be liberated from the cycle of birth and death.

Hinduism is basically polytheistic and many gods and goddesses have been worshiped since the Vedic period. The worship of the Gods and goddesses of Vedic period like Indra, Varuna, Marut, Usha, Aditi and Suryadeva gradually ceased and the worship of the new gods-goddesses began. But one thing is worth remembering that in the entire history of Hinduism, Mahadev Shiva is the only one who has been worshiped since Vedic times. Shiva was called Rudra in the Vedic period and Pashupati during the Indus Valley Civilization. In the excavations of Mohenjo-Daro and Harappa, many pieces of Pashupati figures have been found. Shiva is the only God who is loved by both devas and demons. According to the Ramayana legend, Shri Rama worshiped lord Shiva on the beach of Rameswaram in Tamil Nadu before the attack on Lanka to receive his blessings for victory in the battle against Ravana. Shri Rama's enemy Ravana was also a devotee of Shiva. In this way, Shiva established an ideal of spiritual life in Hinduism. The idol of Shiva portrays him as Mahayogi, Vairagi, who is detached from this illusionary world and engages in meditation without attachment and hatred to anyone and this is why lord shiva is dear to both devas and asura (gods & demons). This is why people called Shiva as Bhole Nath, the kindest God and the Shiva temples are maximum in number all over India.

Lord Shiva is called Mahadeva, Maheshwara or the supreme

God, par brahma (Actual formless God which cannot be perceived by senses), while Lord Shri Rama, Lord Shri Krishna, Lord Buddha and Lord Mahavira were apara Brahms (God in human form). The Supreme Brahman is eternal, infinite, omnipresent, omnipotent, unborn and formless, whereas apara Brahman in human form has many divine attributes, but apar brahma is not eternal and imperishable. Lord Shiva is eternal and immortal; Lord Shri Rama, Lord Krishna, Lord Buddha and Lord Mahavira have left their bodies. The Supreme Brahma is the ultimate truth of the whole world and the essence of the world. Supreme God is the cause of the world, from which the world originates and finally merges into it. That is unique in the supreme God, par brahma.

Shiva is called Rudra in the Vedas. 'Ru' means sorrow and 'Dra' means to liquefy or remove, that is, one who oust sorrow, one who removes the suffering is called Rudra. Shiva means to do welfare, i.e., the eternal Brahman (Supreme Cosmic Spirit) who does welfare to all living beings and removes the sorrow of all beings. This is why Shiva is called Pashupati, that is, the God who is the sole master of all living beings. This is why it is said in the second verse of the third chapter of Shvetashvatara Upanishad -

'Eko hi rudro Na dvitīyāya tasthurya imāṁllokānīśata īśanībhiḥ.
Pratyañjanāṁstiṣṭhati sañcukocāntakāle saṁsṛjya viśvā bhuvanāni gopāḥ.'

He who protects and controls the world by His own powers, He - Rudra - is indeed one only. There is no one beside Him who can make Him the second. Oh men! He is present inside the hearts of all beings. After protecting and maintaining the whole world, He finally withdraws them into Himself.

Saint Tulsi Das writes in the Vinaya Patrika about devotion to Lord Shiva –

'Rishay, siddh, muni, manuj, danuj, sur, apar jeev jag mahi
Tab pad vimukh na par pav kou kalp koti chali jahi'

That is, sages, siddhas, seers, humans, demons, deities and all the creatures of the God cannot overcome the sufferings even after passing millions of kalpas (one kalpa, aeon, is equal to 4.32 billion years) without the blessing of Lord Shiva.

Again, Saint Tulsidas says -

'Bahu kalp upayan Kari anek vina shambhu kripa nahi bhav vivek.'

No matter how many measures would be taken for many kalpas but without the grace of Shiva, there can never be knowledge of the true nature of the world.

Vedas also mentioned Vishnu along with Rudra, but in the ancient legends and mythology, Vishnu has been depicted as a biased God who helps devas and is the enemy of demons. Shri Rama and Shri Krishna who are considered incarnations of Lord Vishnu are not mentioned in the Vedas. The period of both epics namely, Ramayana and Mahabharata are believed to be three thousand to four thousand BC. The worship of Lord Rama and Lord Krishna began after hundreds of years of the composition of both epics. King Rama himself was a devotee of Lord Shiva. Before the attack on Lanka, Shri Rama worshipped lord Shiva at the beach of Rameswaram to take his blessing. Maharishi Sandipani, the guru of Shri Krishna, was a worshiper of Lord Shiva who lived in Avantika (Ujjain).

Ramayana, an ancient epic, was written by Maharishi Valmiki and Ram charit manas was written by Goswami Tulsi Das during medieval period. Both epics have described only about the story of Shri Rama, but in the both Ramayana there is insignificant reference of Ikshvaku or Surya dynasty, whereas the Ikshvaku dynasty needed to be mentioned because Rama's story would be incomplete without discussion of Ikshvaku dynasty. It is to be remembered that there were many great men born in the Ikshvaku dynasty besides Shri Rama whose virtues have left an indelible mark on Indian social and spiritual life. Their deeds were so great that people have remembered them since the time immemorial. In addition to King Ikshvaku in the Ikshvaku dynasty, names of great majestic kings such as Satyavadi Raja Harishchandra, Raja Bhagirath, Raja Dilip and Raja Raghu are notable. Raja Ram's family was called Raghukul. Thus, King Raghu was very majestic, due to which the family of Rama was called Raghukul. Lord Buddha was also born in this Ikshvaku dynasty. According to Ashwaghosha, the author of the 'Buddha Charita' epic, Gautama Buddha's grandfather was the king of the Ikshvaku dynasty who left Ajodhya and built his capital at Kapilavastu. Gautama Buddha was born in Lumbini in 563 BC in the house of King Suddhodana, a Shakya clan of Kshatriya in Ikshvaku dynasty.

The real hero of Mahabharata was Shri Krishna who taught Samkhya, Bhakti and Karma Yoga at the battle field of Mahabharata to Arjun. But it is worth mentioning that in the Mahabharata period, Shri Krishna was not worshiped, but Shri Krishna was considered as a great man. The worship of Shri Krishna began years after the battle of Mahabharata. During the Gupta period during fourth to seventh century, there was a lot of publicity of worship of Shri Krishna. Puranas were composed during the Gupta period, in which Bhagavata Purana describes the life of Shri Krishna. In the Bhagavata Purana, there is a description of Bhagwat story narrated by Maharshi Sukhdev Ji to King Parikshit. King Parikshit was the grandson of Arjuna and son of Abhimanyu. There are eighteen Puranas. The importance of Bhagavata Purana is the highest.

There are many sects in Hinduism among which Shaivism, Vaishnavism, Shakta, Smarta and Saint Sect are prominent. The Shaivite tradition is dominated by Pashupati Shaivism, Kashmiri Shaivite, Siddha, Lingayat, Aghor and Nath sects. Vishnu, Rama, Hanuman, Krishna and Lakshmi are worshiped in the Vaishnava sect. Durga, Kali and other maternal powers are worshiped in the Shakta sect. Apart from the aforesaid sects, Kabir Panth, Dasnami, Arya Samaj, Brahma Samaj, Prarthna Samaj, Ramakrishna Mission, Sai Baba of Shirdi, Radha Swami, Narayan Swami, and many other sects are in Hindu religion. There are differences among the various sects of Hindu due to method of worship and nature of God like corporeal or incorporeal.

During the sixth century BC, there was time of religious reform throughout India, which was led by Gautama Buddha. Due to Vedic religious rituals and customs, the entire society was being exploited by the priests. Hindu society was divided in four Varnas. Varnashrama had created the feeling of high and low in the society, in which Brahmins, Kshatriyas, Vaishyas and Shudras were considered superior and inferior respectively. Even though there was varnashrama in Vedic period but it was based on karma and quality rather than being only as caste form. The son of a Brahmin could also become a Shudra if he had no good karma and virtue and the son of a Shudra could become a Brahmin if he was virtuous. In fact, the Varna system was not by birth during the Vedic period, but was changeable. For this reason, there was no discontent in the society due to Varna system. The Vedic tradition is also mentioned in the Bhagavad Gita. Brahman, Kshatriya, Vaishya and Shudra - These four varnas are grouped on the basis of qualities and deeds. (Bhagavad Gita - 4/13). Again, in chapter eighteen of Bhagavad Gita, from verse forty-one to forty-four, the qualities and deeds of the four varnas have been mentioned. In this Brahmin are those whose conscience is pious, who controls his mind and senses. One who is dedicated for religion, who is devoid of hypocrisy, who is attached to God and one who remains detached from attachment and hatred, happiness and sorrow are the qualities of Brahmin. (Bhagavad Gita - 18/42), bravery, quickness, patience, shrewdness, fearlessness in war and charity are natural qualities of a Kshatriya. (Bhagavad Gita - 18/43), Vaishya has the work of farming, animal husbandry, honest business and serving everyone is job of Shudra. (Bhagavat Gita- 18/44). According to the above interpretation of Bhagavad Gita, karma and inborn qualities were the deciding elements of varnashrama.

Varnashrama was based on karma and qualities in the Vedic period but it took the form of caste in the later Vedic period. The Brahmins who were considered an ideal of virtues in the Vedic period became hypocrites, ritualistic and exploiters of society in the later Vedic period. The whole society started going down to immorality. Society was tormented by the exploitation of priests. Kshatriyas used to perform sacrifices to attain heaven in which many animals were sacrificed. The whole society was wandering in the darkness of ignorance. Now religion had become a business of hypocrites, swindlers and fraud. Due to the practice of sacrifice of animals, human beings became selfish, insensitive and violent.

Indra, the king of the Vedic deities, was depicted as a lecherous, conspirator, power hungry, dubious, jealous who used to spoil the austerities of ascetics through the nymph (apsara) of Indraloka. Devraj Indra's character also had an impact on the people and they too started adopting corrupt practices by taking inspiration from Indra. The whole society was going down.

In the midst of such darkness, a great man emerged, whom the famous English writer Sir Edwin Arnold called 'Light of Asia'. It is said that- 'When the earth becomes restless and agony surrounds everywhere, the great men came on the earth as messiah to save the people from sufferings.'

2
RISE OF BUDDHISM

Siddhartha Gautama, the founder of Buddhism, was born in 543 BC. He was son of Suddhodana, the king of Kapilavastu, a Republican state of Nepal. Maharaja Suddhodana wanted to make his son an emperor. But Siddhartha Gautama was born to cure the sufferings of all human beings. Before the birth of Siddhartha Gautama, Asita, a great ascetic of the Himalayan had seen through his inner vision that in the house of King Suddhodana a messiah would be born who would show the path to all human beings to overcome their sufferings. At the time of the birth of Siddhartha Gautama, some astrologer had also predicted that this child would not be a king or an emperor but he would be a great seer. Due to this prediction, King Suddhodana made all efforts so that Siddhartha Gautama's mind gets entangled in the worldliness. King Suddhodana made a lot of arrangements for Siddhartha's comforts and luxuries. He got made three beautiful palaces for Siddhartha for the three seasons. He made all arrangements for dancing and singing there. But all these things could not keep Siddhartha tied up in the world. One day Siddharth Gautama went out to visit the garden. He saw an old man on the street who was staggering on the road due to his old age. The old man was walking slowly on the road and trembling with a stick in his hand. The second time he saw a patient whose eyes had turned yellow, the face was wilted and was having trouble in breathing and he was only able to walk with the help of another person. For the third time Siddhartha saw a dead person who was carried in a coffin by four persons. There were many people behind the funeral procession. Some were crying, some were beating their chests, these scenes distracted Siddhartha a lot. He saw that this world is full of sorrow. Every man in this world is sad for some reason. This world is full of sufferings due to old age, disease, death of someone in the family and many types of mental afflictions. Having seen the condition of human life, he got disillusioned. Despite king Suddhodana's efforts, Siddhartha Gautama, at the age of 29, gave up luxuries and comforts of a princely life and left the palace with his chariot driver without telling anyone in the palace and went towards the forest. Siddharth Gautama well understood that this world is full of sorrow but he wanted to find the answer to the question, what is the root cause of the suffering of man and what is the way to get rid of this sorrow?

After leaving his home, Siddhartha Gautama first reached Vaishali (Bihar) where he met Acharya Alara Kalama, a scholar of Samkhya philosophy. Siddharth Gautama stayed in the ashram of Acharya Alara Kalama and learnt yoga and meditation from him, but the teaching of Acharya Alara Kalama could not answer Gautam's questions. After this, with the permission of his Guru, he went ahead and reached the Rajagriha, where he met Rudraka Ramputra, the great scholar of that time and by staying in his ashram, Siddhartha Gautama got spiritual knowledge from him. Even the teachings of Acharya Rudraka Ramputra could not answer the original questions of Siddharth Gautama. One day after taking permission from his teacher, Acharya Rudraka Ramputra, he set out towards the forest of Uruvela (Bodh Gaya), where he found Koundilya and other four sanyasis who became first disciples of Gautama Buddha after his enlightenment.

After intensive meditation for six years, at the age of 35, Siddhartha Gautama received enlightenment on the night of Baisakh Purnima during deep meditation under a Peepal tree (sacred fig) on the bank of the Niranjana River. After his enlightenment, Siddhartha became famous in the world as Gautama Buddha and Tathagata. Buddha means the destruction of the ignorance and the attainment of supreme wisdom and the Tathagata means liberation from the cycle of birth and death.

Again, a question arises, what knowledge did Siddhartha Gautama gained during meditation in Bodh Gaya? The obvious answer to this question is that he got answer to all questions for which he had left his palace that is, what is the root cause of human suffering and what is the way to get rid of this suffering? Buddha found the answer to all these questions during his meditation. In addition to this, Buddha saw his past lives as well as cosmic reality of the nature of this universe and the nature of human being's mind. Buddha got answers to many curiosities during this meditation.

Siddhartha Gautama initially started practice of sadhana in the old ways by renouncing the food but as a result, his health began to decline rapidly. One day he fell unconscious. In the meantime, he heard a song which meant "Don't let the lute (veena) strings loose. Leaving loose, it will not be able to produce melodious voice and don't tighten the wires so much that it breaks." He agreed that yoga could only be practiced by proper dieting. Extreme is not good for anything. The middle path is best way to achieve any goal. Gautama Buddha gave up the old ways of sadhana and researched many new ways. He devoted his entire life to meditation and discovered many ways and techniques of meditation by which a man can know everything, that is, the truth of this universe. Everything is contained in this infinite universe.

In the beginning, Siddhartha Gautama through intense meditation removed the knots of unwholesome things lying in the dormant state in the subconscious mind since many past lives. It should be remembered that in the subconscious mind, sensual feelings, anger, greed, ego, worldly attachments, hatred and other types of defilements are usually stored in a passive state which are hindrances in the way of enlightenment. Many types of dormant defilements in subconscious mind usually come in the dreams. The memory of the past events and the evil karma done by man remains in subconscious mind in the same way as the old files are kept in the computer. When the mind is concentrated, old things come to the mind. That is why it is said that good conduct is the first condition for doing yoga and meditation.

Siddhartha Gautama got success in removing all the unwholesome thoughts from his mind through continuous practice of meditation. Unwholesome things of mind are the biggest obstacle in the path of attainment of enlightenment. Siddhartha Gautama's mind became completely clean. When the garbage dumped in subconscious mind is eliminated, then the mind gets cleaned. Then the feeling of divinity such as joy, friendliness, compassion, gratitude, nonviolence, wisdom, peace, truth and charity start sprouting in the mind.

Siddharth Gautama got his mind purified. Now he had to proceed further for his last destination. Through subtle meditation, he elevated his consciousness at the highest level where a sadhaka comes to know about the past, the future and the present as well as many mysteries of the universe. There is complete destruction of illusion, ignorance and finally enlightenment is achieved.

Siddhartha Gautama meditated deeply on the mid night of Baisakh Purnima. He saw everything in this universe. All things in the universe are made up of molecules. Every creature on the earth is just an organism of invisible molecules. Human beings are not aware of their true nature and are wandering in ignorance. Everything in this universe is changeable and mortal. Only the form of the living being changes. Childhood, youth, old age and death, and then the endless cycle of birth-death goes on in every living being. Siddhartha Gautama noticed his many past births in meditation. Siddhartha Gautama got answers to all the questions for which he had left his palace. He saw that this world is full of suffering. The reason for suffering is man's attachment to the worldly things, that is, the craving is the main cause of sorrow that arises due to ignorance. He saw that because of attachment, the cycle of birth and death goes on. The cycle of birth and death continues in this way - 1-Avidya, 2-Sanskara (instinct), 3-Science (consciousness), 4-Nāmrup (The meaning of the nama is mind + rupa means body, made of five material substances.), 5-Shadayatana (five senses and mind), 6- Sparsh, (Touch, contact with external subjects), 7-Vedana (sensation), 8-Trishna (attachment), 9-Upadana (intense desire to live), 10- Bhava (this world), 11-Jati (rebirth) and 12-Jāra (Death. These twelve interlinked journeys from Avidya to Jara keeps happening one after the other, which is called the principle of cause and effect or Pratityasamutpada. It is 'Asmin sati idam bhavati' that means it happens. The whole nature is bound by the subtle and invisible chain of cause and effect, that is, the life of human being is bound by good and bad karma (deeds). Thus, the cycle of endless birth and death goes on. Freedom from this cycle of birth-death can be attained only by nirvana after dispelling the ignorance.

Gautama Buddha discovered the eightfold path for the diagnosis of suffering and advised people to follow the ashtanga path for the relief from the sorrow. Gautama Buddha asked to follow the five moral codes, i.e., Panchsheela before following the ashtanga path.

The basic moral code of conduct (Panchsheela) in Buddhism is 1. Do not commit violence, 2. Do not steal, 3. Do not commit adultery, 4. Do not lie, 5. Do not intoxicate.

Gautam Buddha said that every person in this world is unhappy due to some cause. *There are four noble truths, namely,*

1. *There is suffering in world.*
2. *There is reason for suffering.*
3. *The suffering can be prevented.*
4. *There is the way to get relief from the suffering.*

The basic elements of the *eight-fold path of Buddha* are -

1. *Right vision: (Samyak Drishti) means seeing as it is. Do not bring any of your prejudices in between. Accept anything after proper investigation and examination, in short, scientific and logical thinking is called right vision.*
2. *Right Resolution: Continuous efforts for mental and moral development.*
3. *Right speech: no false and hateful speech and writing.*
4. *Righteous Karma: Don't do harmful deeds which are injurious to others.*

5. *Right livelihood: Do not do any expressly or implicitly harmful business.*
6. *Right Effort: Try to improve oneself.*
7. *Right memory: Developing mental ability to see with clear vision.*
8. *Right meditation (Samyak Samadhi): Continuous practice of meditation to attain nirvana.*

After attaining enlightenment, Gautama Buddha gave his first sermon at Mrigdava (Sarnath) near Varanasi and the first five sadhaka became his followers who had left Siddhartha Gautama because he had given up the path of fasting. Gautama Buddha went on propagating Buddhism in Pali, a lingua franca of that time till the age of eighty. The popularity of his scientific, clear and simple religion began to grow rapidly.

Buddhists used to chant the mantras of three refuge, Trisharan i.e., 'Buddhaam Sharanam Gachhami, Dhammam Sharanam Gachhami, Sangham Sharanam Gachhami.'

The word Buddha means: awakened, enlightened person. This word does not mean a person but it is directed to convey an enlightenment. Even before Gautama Buddha, many people have got enlightenment and in the future, any sadhaka can attain enlightenment. The highest wisdom is the state of enlightenment where all human weaknesses disappear. The enlightened person acquires all divine qualities like God. Historian H.G. Wells states that Gautama Buddha never talked about God, but all his qualities were of the divine.

Dhamma means: Dhamma or Dharma does not mean cult, but the search for eternal truth. The great codes of life, from which the whole existence is going on. The Chinese Saint Lhotse called this 'Tao'. Buddha called it 'Dhamma' in Pali language.

Sangha means: the association of seekers of truth, the group of the seekers engaged in meditation, those who want to awaken their consciousness at the highest level and a journey of self-discovery. Those who want to dispel their ignorance and get out of the cycle of birth and death.

Buddhists called Buddha as their greatest teacher, guide and Lord.

They believe that Bhagwan is basically a Pali word, which is made up of Bhag and Van. 'Bhagna' means to destroy, and 'van' means cravings. The person who has destroyed all his craving is called Bhagwan.

Gautama Buddha was opposed to caste and gender inequality which was prevailing in the society between high and low caste and between man and woman. According to Buddha all human beings are equal. There were Brahmins, Kshatriyas, Vaishyas and Shudras among his disciples who lived together and there was no discrimination between them. There is a legend in Buddhist literature that two Brahmins named Vatsya and Bhardwaja went to Buddha and told him that there was a dispute between them about, whether a person becomes Brahmin by birth or by karma. Answering this question Buddha replied – Oh, Vatsya and Bharadwaj! The man who grazes the cows in the grass land is called a herdsman - not a Brahmin. The person who makes his living from art, we call him an artist - not a Brahmin, a man who does another's job will be called a servant - not a Brahmin, he who steals will be called a thief - not a Brahmin, a man who works in the army - he is called a soldier - not a Brahmin. No one born from the womb of a particular mother will be called Brahmin, but a person who has no attachment to anything - I will call him a Brahmin. He who has cut off all his bonds and got himself separated from attachment-hatred and who does not get distracted in every situation - I will call him a Brahmin. One who is free from anger, who does good deeds, who speaks the truth, who has conquered his desires - I will call him a Brahmin. In fact, neither one is a Brahmin by being born in a Brahmin's family nor non-Brahmin by not being born in non-Brahmin family. By one's action and quality anyone becomes a Brahmin and the other a non-Brahmin. The person becomes farmer, craftsman, businessman or a servant by his work and not by birth.

Gautama Buddha always remained silent on the question of God and he did not think it appropriate to answer this question because it would create many misconceptions. He said that our life is regulated by our actions and there is no intervention of God or external power in it. Human suffering arises due to ignorance in the life and God will never remove our sorrows unless we live consciously. That is why Buddha used to repeatedly emphasize modesty i.e., good character in life, wisdom i.e., knowledge and meditation or vipassana. He used to tell a story that if a traveller is injured on the road by a poisoned arrow, will we save him first, treat him by removing the poisoned arrow from his body or let him die by discussing needless matters like who killed him or from which direction did the arrow come? Who was the arrow bearer? Was he soldier or a civilian? Was he white or black? Was he tall or short? If we lose the crucial time on the debate on needless questions, we will not be able to save that person.

Lord Buddha's purpose of the above 'poisonous arrow' story was that people should not misuse the valuable time of limited life in imaginary and mystic questions rather they should make their lives better through good character, wisdom and meditation and move towards the goal of attaining nirvana.

Once, Ananda asked Gautama Buddha - Hey Buddha! Why does every person not attain enlightenment? Then Buddha smiled and told Ananda to go and ask people of some villages and towns about their desires in life. On Buddha's order, Ananda went from house to house in many villages and townships and asked people what were their desires in this life. Someone told Ananda that he had only daughters, now he had a desire for a son. Someone told that he needed a government job. Someone told Ananda that he needed a lot of money. Someone told that he needed a government post. Someone told that his enemies should be destroyed. No person told Ananda that he was desirous to get enlightenment, rather they didn't know anything about enlightenment or nirvana.

When Ananda returned from his journey, he narrated everything to Buddha, then Buddha smiled and said, now you understood what the wishes of the people are? When a man does not have the desire for enlightenment and nirvana then why will he try in this direction? Buddha told Ananda that in reality man is so attached to worldly things that he is not aware of self-knowledge or nirvana. The man is going blindly in a state of unconsciousness.

Lord Buddha said to Ananda that Oh, Ananda! There are four types of people in this world, - the first are those who are moving from darkness to darkness. The second are those who are going from light to darkness. The third type of people are those who are going from darkness to light and the fourth are moving from light to light. Lord Buddha explained the above sentences and said that there are people of the first type who are suffering due to their past and present bad karma. They have lecherous desire, anger, fear, greed and other types of evils, but they do not make any effort to get rid of the misery or ignorance and die living in ignorance.

The second type of people are those who are born in a well-to-do family. They have wealth and power, but they become egoistic and characterless due to wealth and power and start doing immoral karma. They waste their future by denigrating their character and doing bad deeds. They are bound to reap the fruits of their bad karma in this life or next life.

The third are those who go from darkness to light. If a man was involved in wrong deeds due to ignorance, but afterward he began to realize that his path was not right and he keeps trying to improve himself and continue to be good.

The fourth type of people are those who are born with good values and by creating the right vision in their life, they try to reach up to the spiritual height through modesty, meditation and knowledge and ultimately, they achieve nirvana by attaining enlightenment.

Gautama Buddha was against all kinds of superstition or blind faith of the people. While preaching at one place, he said, imagine that the Achiravati River is full of water. On the other side of the river there is a man who wants to come to this side of the river for some work. If the man standing on that side of the river prays that the other side of the river should come to him, or prays to Indra, Varuna, Brahma or Vishnu or by chanting the mantras that Oh, God! Make me cross the river without swimming or without going by a boat, then that person would be called a fool. Just as by praying that man cannot come across the river, in the same way no man can get rid of bad karma of his life by offering yagnas or rituals or animal sacrifices or by chanting mantras. Every man has to do good deeds to get his salvation.

Gautama Buddha advised people to think logically and scientifically and not to accept anything which is irrational. He advised the people to weigh any matter or do test on the anvil of wisdom before accepting any matter. Buddha's advice described as Kalama Sutta in the Anguttara nikaya of Sutta Pitaka is called Charter of Free Inquiry.

Once Gautama Buddha, also known as Shakya Muni, was passing through the Keshavpur area along with his monks, then the people of Kalama tribe saw him and humbly requested him to sit on the pedestal. After serving him, the chief of the Kalama tribe said to the Buddha - Oh Buddha! You are a great sage. Only you can solve our doubts. Many religious preachers come to our area and they describe their religion as good and criticized other religions. This creates confusion in our mind. We want to know which religion should be followed. Kindly remove our doubts and clear our confusion.

Gautama Buddha told Kalama tribe that don't believe on anything that has been repeatedly said, because by repeating the lie again and again it seems to be true. Do not accept any opinion or thing coming from the tradition, because many social evils are followed by the people from centuries.

Do not go by any rumour or what is said in any religious scripture or said by any monk or has been followed by many people. Buddha said that before accepting anything, opinion or religion, adopt some yardstick and examine them on those criteria then you will find the right path.

Following criterion or yardstick suggested by Lord Buddha in Kalama Sutta: -

1. *If that opinion, thought or religion produces purity, non-violence and happiness in the mind.*
2. *If it is in the welfare of oneself and in the interest of public.*
3. *Which does not create feelings of violence, maliciousness, hatred and bitterness.*

4. *Which seems to be right after proper examination through prudent mind.*
5. *That which is proved right by one's own discovery or experience.*
6. *Which creates a feeling of love, compassion and harmony.*
7. *Which is free from confusion, hypocrisy and superstition.*

Many scholars and philosophers in Europe and other western countries have praised the said Kalama Sutta of Gautama Buddha and said that cults, religion or any idea should be evaluated on basis of criterion suggested by Buddha in Kalama sutta.

After attaining enlightenment at Bodh Gaya, Gautama Buddha continued to inspire the people in Bihar and eastern Uttar Pradesh to attain nirvana by following the path of knowledge. In each of his discourses, he described purity of conduct (modesty), meditation and knowledge as the main elements of religion and said that by following this path the salvation is possible. He said that right vision will be created only when the mind is pure and the mind will be pure only when meditation is practiced continuously. It is possible to attain enlightenment only by meditation.

At Kushinagar (Eastern Uttar Pradesh), Lord Buddha said to the monks at the age of 80 before his death – 'hey monks! The journey of my life is going to end now. Now you become your own lamp. Delusion, lies and ignorance are everywhere in this world. Detach yourself from them and go into meditation. The nirvana is possible only through meditation practice. Forget the past, because it is not going to return, the future is uncertain, just stay in the present and don't waste your time. Always keep in mind that this world is impermanent and your life is also temporary. Therefore, do not waste this life in vain'.

Gautama Buddha's ideology had so much impact throughout India that during the reign of Emperor Ashoka, Buddhism spread throughout India from Afghanistan to Burma and its neighbouring countries. The first Buddhist Council was held in the Rajgriha soon after the death of Buddha under the patronage of Emperor Ajatshatru of Magadha in which eleven hundred senior monks participated. The biggest achievement of that conference was that two important

Pitakas of Buddhism namely, Vinaya Pitaka and Sutta Pitaka were composed in it. Vinaya Pitaka is a collection of the code of conduct for organisation and monks and Sutta Pitaka is a collection of discourses of Gautama Buddha. Abhidhamma Pitaka was composed in the second Buddhist Council which was held in Vaishali. Abhidhamma Pitaka discusses Buddhist philosophy. Thus, Tripitakas are the great texts of Buddhism. In Buddhist literature, 'Dhammapada' occupies the same place as the Bhagavad Gita in Hinduism and holy Bible in Christianity. The Dhammapada is part of the Khuddak nikaya of Sutta Pitaka. It has a collection of teachings of Lord Buddha which is in Pali language and is divided into 26 chapters and 423 verses.

Emperor Ashoka had sent his son, prince Mahendra and daughter, princess Sanghamitra to Sri Lanka and some other countries of the south East Asia for the promotion of Buddhism, due to which Buddhism spread in those countries. Emperor Ashoka propagated Buddhism by inscribing the main principles of Buddhism on stone pillars. Buddhism remained the main religion of India for almost one thousand years. Emperor Bimbisara, King Prasenjit of Kosala, Emperor Ajatshatru, Emperor Ashoka, Emperor Kanishka, king Melinda, Emperor Harshavardhana and King Dharmapala of Pala dynasty played major role in the propagation of Buddhism. Around 640 AD, the last Buddhist emperor was Harshavardhana, who after every four years used to distribute his treasury money for public welfare and himself lived the life of a monk. Around the first century the Indo-Greek king Millender or Melinda was a Buddhist whose kingdom extended from Afghanistan to Punjab in north-western India. The conversation between King Millender and the Buddhist monk Nagasena is stored in 'Milindapanho' (Question of Melinda), a major text of Buddhism in the Pali language, which is believed to have been compiled around first century AD. In this book many questions related to Buddhism have been discussed.

Many scholars, philosophers, kings and emperors became Buddhists and followed the philosophy of Buddha, but those notable monks who got enlightenment by listening and realizing the thoughts of Buddha are SariPutra, Moggallana, Mahakashyap, Subhuti, Purna Maitrayi putra, Katyayana, Anuradha, Upali and Ananda.

Even today, Buddhists are spread in many countries. Buddhism is the fourth largest religion in the world in terms of numbers. The special feature of this religion is that it has spread due to its logical and scientific philosophy. Even today educated people of world are getting influenced towards Buddhism, because the main theme of this religion is meditation, knowledge and purity of conduct. Unlike many other religions, this religion has not been propagated by the help of sword, violence, fear and greed, but because of its philosophical elements. But unfortunately, this scientific religion disappeared from India where it was born. On this point, the famous poet Allama Iqbal states that-

'Qaum ne paiġhām-e-gautam kī zarā parvā na kī
Qadr pahchānī Na apne gauhar-e-yak-dāna kī
Aah bad-qismat rahe āvāz-e-haq se be-ḳhabar
Ġhāfil apne phal kī shīrīnī se hotā hai shajar
Āshkār us ne kiyā jo zindagī kā raaz thā
Hind ko lekin ḳhayālī falsafa par naaz thā
Sham-e-haq se jo munavvar ho ye vo mahfil na thī
Bārish-e-rahmat huī lekin zamīñ qābil na thī.'

Allama Iqbal says that the people of India did not care at all for the messages of Gautama Buddha. This country did not consider the value of its only diamond. Alas! How unfortunate this country is? Gautama Buddha put the ultimate truth in front of everyone which was yet unknown to the people. That truth by which a man can get rid of suffering. How to get rid of the cycle of birth and death? How to get out of the darkness of ignorance and go towards the light of knowledge? How to make unhappy life blissful with meditation and wisdom, and how to conquer the mind and own senses?

But this messiah who told the ultimate truth was forgotten and once again the people of India got trapped in castes, hypocrisy, ritualism, falsehood and priesthood which took the life towards darkness. The people of India forgot their own precious diamond but today India's identity in the world is due to Buddha. Lakhs of people from many countries visit the Buddhist memorial sites of India every year and take the soil of India with devotion to their country.

3
JAINISM

Jainism is very ancient religion of India. The 'Jain' word derives from 'Jin' that means to conquer, to conquer over own senses and mind. The person who has conquered over his senses is called Jeetendra, Jina, Nirgrantha or Arihant. Jainism has the tradition of living an ascetic life. The five codes of conducts, such as truth, non-violence, aparigraha i.e., not to accumulate more property than necessary, asteya i.e., not to grab or steal other's wealth and celibacy have to be followed in Jainism.

Although there are total of 24 Tirthankaras in Jainism, the name of the 24th and last Tirthankara is most famous. Tirthankara is a person who has conquered over the cycle of death and rebirth and made a path for others to follow. The first Tirthankara was King Rishabhdeva and 23rd Tirthankara was Parshvanath, the son of King Ashvasen of Varanasi. Mahavir Swami, the last and the 24th Tirthankara of Jainism was born in a Kshatriya royal family in Kundal village of Vaishali (Bihar) in 599 BC. His father's name was King Siddhartha. Vardhman Mahavira became disenchanted with the world at the age of 30 and left the royal palace and took ascetic life. After 12 years of hard meditation and penance, he attained Kaivalya and after that he started propagating religion. The soul of Mahavir Swami left his body at the age of 72 in Pavapuri (Bihar). The eleven persons who first got the sermons from lord Mahavira were called Ganadhara, the main disciples. Indrabhuti was first among them.

In Jainism non-violence has been considered the main tenet of religion. Swami Mahavira while teaching his monks said that they should make such efforts with mind, words and deeds so that no creature can suffer. Monks should always be alert while speaking, walking, getting up, eating or resting so that no harm is caused to any creature. He used to put stress on getting the victory over the senses, mind and action. He said that it is a sin to have bad thoughts in the mind.

Lord Mahavira used to ask his disciples to do good karma. He used to say that everyone has to bear the fruits of his good and bad actions in this life or in the next life. Jainism does not believe in the authority of God but puts stress on the austerity. The highest state of self-development is considered as divine state. Like Hinduism, Buddhism and Sikhism, Jainism considers salvation as the ultimate goal of human life, that is, liberation from the cycle of birth and death is the ultimate goal of life.

Jainism believes that this entire creation is made up of six elements or substances like Soul (Jiva or Jeevatma), Matter (Pudgal) i.e., combination of physical matter or molecules, Motion & Rest (Dharma & Adharma), Space (Akash) and Time (Kaal). According to Jainism, this universe has always existed and will remain in existence. This universe is controlled by natural law through the process of its own energy. Jainism believes that the universe is eternal and God or another person has not created it.

Jain philosophy says that by following right knowledge, right philosophy and right character a person can get rid of his karmic bondage and attain salvation. About karma bondage, it can be said in simple language that it is impossible to get rid of the cycle of birth and death without paying the account of the deeds done by a person. Due to karma bondage a person is born again and again in some creature. According to Jainism by following right knowledge, right philosophy and right character a person can get rid of karma bondage.

Jainism considers the four kashayas (hindrance) as the main cause of human sufferings which crop up due to ignorance. These four kashayas are, Anger, Ego (ahankara), Delusion (maya) and Greed. The end of these kashayas is necessary for salvation. To keep these four kashayas under the control, one should follow the path of mediation, compassion and friendliness. Eighteen types of sins have been described in Jainism namely, Violence, theft, self-gratification, cruelty, extra marital relationship, false accusation, attachment, malice, accumulating excessive wealth, false philosophy, malpractices, delusion, greed, discord, anger, ego, false speech etc. All these sins have very bad consequences.

In the third century AD, Jainism got divided into two sects. At that time, there was a severe famine in Pataliputra (Patna) due to which Acharya Bhadrabahu went to South India with thousands of Jain monks and stayed for twelve years in Shravanabelagola, Karnataka. He then returned to Pataliputra with Jain monks. When he arrived here, he saw that under the leadership of Acharya Sthulabahu, thousands of Jain monks were wearing white clothes. According to Jain tradition, Jain monks used to live without clothes, Digambara. So, the issue of clothes and without clothes was deepened and Jainism got divided into two sects. Acharya Bhadrabahu was the leader of the Digambar monks and Sthulavahu was the leader of the Svetambara Sanyasis.

Jainism does not accept caste system which is similar to Buddhism. Jain texts state that the true Brahmin is the one who has overcome attachment, hatred and fear and keeps his senses under control.

All the Tirthankaras of Jainism were born in Kshatriya families, due to this, many Kshatriya kings, Maharajas and emperors were the followers of Jainism. Jainism was accepted by the emperor Chandragupta, King Kharvela of Kalinga, the kings of Rashtrakutas and Chalukya of South India.

The 'Tattvartha sutra' composed by Jain Acharya Umaswamy is considered to be the sacred epic of all sects of Jainism. It is also called 'tattva-learning-sutra' and 'moksha-shastra'. Its composition period is believed to be of the second century AD. There are ten chapters and 350 sutras in this book written in Sanskrit language. The chapters are as follows: - 1-Faith and Knowledge, 2-The Category of the Living,

3-The Lower World and the Middle World, 4-The Celestial Beings, 5-The Category of the Non-Living, 6-Influx of Karma, 7-The Five Vows, 8-Bondage of Karma, 9-Stoppage & Shedding of Karma, 10-Liberation.

The first sutra of chapter one of the Tattvartha Sutra- "Samyagdarshana gyanacharitrani moksamarga" means - Samyak Darshan (Right View), Samyak Jnana (Right knowledge) and Samyak Charitra (Right conduct) together all lead to the path to salvation. Samyak Darshan means seeing as it is. Do not bring any of self-conceived notion or prejudices in between. To accept anything after thorough examination, in short, scientific thinking is called right philosophy.

"Prasparopgraha jeevanam, i.e Mutual Cooperation Jeevanam" This sutra is the motto of Jainism. It is written at the end of the Jain emblem. It means, to reciprocate each other is the duty or religion of every living being. (Tattvartha Sutra- 5.21)

4
SIKHISM

Sikh means teachings. The teachings imparted by the Gurus subsequently became the foundation of Sikhism. Sikhism is the new religion among all religions. It was founded by Guru Nanak Dev, who was born at the bank of Ravi River in the year 1465 on the day of Kartik Purnima at Talwandi in Punjab of Pakistan. His father's name was Mr. Kaluchand Khatri and mother's name was shrimati Tripta Devi. His wife's name was Sulakshana Devi. Guru Nanak Dev died at the age of 70 at Kartar Pur in Pakistan.

Guru Nanak was interested in spiritual subjects from his childhood and he used to listen to the sermons of saints and fakirs. He was not interested in worldly matters and always used to meditate on the spiritual subjects. Although he was in family life and had two sons but from the very beginning, he was detached from the worldly subjects.

At the age of thirty-five along with his four spiritual companions, Mardana, Lahna, Bala and Ramdas he travelled to many important religious places and shared his spiritual thoughts among people. Gradually, the people started getting influenced by his spiritual thoughts.

Guru Nanak used to say that God is one and he is formless. He further said that as the water is one but the name of water is different in every country, similarly God is one but he is called by different names in every religion. Guru Nanak considered idol worship, ostentation, Varna system, religious rituals and priesthood to be inappropriate and emphasized on the friendliness with all religions. Guru Nanak used to emphasize on human equality. He used to say that the differences among the human beings arise due to egoism. Guru Nanak Dev used to say that God should always be remembered and hatred with any creature would be similar to disliking the God's creations.

After the death of Guru Nanak, the tradition of Guru started in Sikhism. Guru Nanak was followed by Guru Angad, Guru Amardas, Guru Ramdas, Guru Arjun Dev, Guru Har Govind Singh, Guru Har Rai, Guru Har Kishan, Guru Tegh Bahadur and Guru Govind Singh respectively. After the last Guru Govind Singh, the Guru tradition was abolished and Guru Granth Saheb was considered as a Guru. Thus, there are ten Gurus in Sikhism.

Guru Granth saheb, the holiest book of Sikhism was composed by Guru Arjun Dev but its final form was given by the tenth Guru, Guru Govind Singh. In Guru Granth Sahib, along with the verses of Sikh Gurus, the verses of Saint Kabir, Saint Ramanand, Sufi Saint Baba Farid, Saint Namdev, Saint Ravidas, Saint Dhanna and Saint Surdas are also compiled.

A grand Gurudwara - Harmandir Saheb was got built by the fourth Sikh Guru Ramdas in Amritsar city of Punjab province, which is known as the Golden Temple. It is called Darbar Saheb i.e., the court of God which is the spiritual centre of Sikhism. Tourists from all over the country and people of all religions come here to pray and to listen to the sweet Guru Vani to purify their mind.

Central Principles of Sikhism -

1. *God is one. An Onkar called by Sikhs as 'Waheguru' means God is the supreme master and teacher.*
2. *Everything in the world is done by the desire of God, but due to ignorance one does not realize it.*
3. *Speak the truth and never take the side of falsehood.*
4. *To cleanse the mind, serve all living beings and pray to God.*
5. *A - chanting the name of God - listening about God, contemplating about God and meditating on God, (Nidhidhyasana).*

   B - Kirat - earn livelihood through hard labour and honesty. Do not steal or cheat.

C – Band Chakhna – Apart from maintenance of own family do some charitable works with the money earned. The langar in gurudwaras is run by this spirit.

6. *Sabat bhala: Think about the welfare of all beings and do good deeds.*
7. *Be careful of five thieves – sexual desire, anger, greed, attachment and ego, these are the five thieves who steal the peace and purity of the mind and spoil the good karma.*
8. *Hatred in the name of caste and religion is the cause of sufferings. There should not be any kind of discrimination. There should be no discrimination between men and women. In Sikhism, by removing caste surnames, all men have been instructed to use 'Singh' and 'Kaur' as surnames for women.*
9. *Sikhism denounces superstition, ritualism, hypocrisy and priesthood as untrue and advised Sikhs to stay away from all these blind faiths.*
10. *Five Rules for Sikhs-*

In Sikhism, it is necessary for men to keep head hair, wearing bracelet in hand, comb, kutchh (under garment) and the sword. Hair is a symbol of faith to God, bracelet is symbol of fearlessness, comb stands for the purity of mind and body, Kuccha for self-restraint and celibacy and sword stands for self-defence, fearlessness and awareness against injustice.

There are many sects in Sikhism, namely, Uddasi, Nirmal, Nanakpanthi, Khalsa, Sahajdhari, Namdhari, Kuka, Nirankari and Sarwariya.

5
JUDAISM

In ancient time, polytheism was prevalent all over the world. In the ancient civilizations of Mesopotamia (Iraq), Assyria, Egypt and Greece people worshiped nature along with many deities, but in West Asia around fifteen hundred BC with the birth of the Abrahamic religion, the old practice of worship of many deities started decreasing. In the countries of West Asia, Europe and Africa, with the birth of Judaism, Christianity and Islam, the old religious system gradually came to an end.

The religion which first came in the west Asia is called Abrahamic religion. This religion was founded by Hasrat Abraham. Abraham is considered to be the first Prophet of the three important religions of the world i.e., Judaism, Christianity and Islam and these religions are called Abrahamic religions.

Hasrat Abraham was born around fifteen hundred BC at a place called Ur of ancient Babylonia (Iraq). His father's name was Tarah. Abraham had three wives, whose names were Sarah, Hagar and Keturah. Abraham had eight sons. Ishmael was born from Abraham's second wife, while Isaac was born from his first wife, Sarah and the other six sons were born from Keturah. Many generations of Abraham, from Abraham to Moses are considered prophets of Judaism, Christianity and Islam. The name of the grandson of Abraham was Yaqub or Israel, after whom the country of Israel was named.

It is said that Abraham's father was a trader of idols. In those days, idol worship and polytheism were prevalent everywhere. Abraham thought it was wrong to worship idol and he used to say that God is one and is formless. He justified the monotheistic theory of one God and made his religion against idol worship. After some time, Abraham left Ur city and moved to Canaan (Israel) but in the meantime there was a severe famine in Canaan due to which Abraham left Canaan and went to Egypt where he had to live like a vagabond. He and his descendants had to become the slave of the pharaoh, but after a few years, they left Egypt and again moved to Canaan (Israel), where the descendants of Abraham ruled. After living for over one hundred years, Abraham died in Hebron in Palestine.

Though Judaism was started by Prophet Abraham, but the actual Messiah of Judaism was Moses, who was the descendant of Prophet Abraham. It is said that Abraham's descendants faced many difficulties and slavery of the pharaoh of Egypt, but Moses saved the Jewish race. Because of this, the prestige of Prophet Moses is the highest in Judaism. It was Moses who laid the foundation of Jewish rule in Israel.

It said that during the meditation, Hasrat Moses got instructions from the God to follow Ten Commandments which became the *laws of Judaism. 10 Commandments are as follows -*

1. *You will not worship any other deity besides me (God).*
2. *You will not worship any of my pictures or idols.*
3. *You will not take the name of God without reason.*
4. *The seventh day, i.e., the day of Swathe will be kept holy.*
5. *You will respect your parents.*
6. *You will not kill anyone.*
7. *You will not have illegitimate physical relation with anyone.*
8. *You will not steal.*
9. *You will not give false testimony*
10. *You will not damage the other's property jealously.*

The Jewish people call God in Hebrew language as 'Yahweh' who is abstract, formless, omnipresent, just, loving, compassionate and strict. He punishes if his orders are violated. The main text of the

Jews is the 'Torah', a group of the first five texts of the Bible, called the Old Testament.

Jews are very few in the entire world and forty percent of its total population lives in Israel and the rests are spread in other European countries and America. Though this religion is followed by less in terms of population, however the importance of this religion is due to the reason that two important religions of the world i.e., Christianity and Islam have originated from this religion. Prophet of Judaism is considered prophet of Christian and Islam religions.

6
CHRISTIANITY

Christianity is an Abrahamic religion which is monotheistic. The followers of Christianity consider Jesus as their most revered Messiah, but the Jewish do not consider Jesus as prophet and say that no other Messiah after Moses is yet born into the Abrahamic religion. Jewish say that there is still a big time left for the Messiah to be born.

The teachings of Jesus Christ are compiled in the New Testament of the Bible. Even in Christianity, it is necessary to follow the Ten Commandments of Judaism. Christianity accepts the Trinity as God, that is, God as the Father, His son Jesus Christ and the Holy Spirit.

Jesus Christ, the prophet of Christianity, was born at a village called Nazareth, ten kilometres south from Jerusalem, which was part of the Roman Empire under the Galilee province in those days. His father's name was Joseph, who was Jewish and worked as a carpenter. His mother's name was Mary (Maryam). According to Christianity, at the time of Jesus's arrival in Mary's womb, Mary was a virgin. So, the Christian considered Mary as virgin mother and Jesus Christ as a divine son.

Since his youth, Jesus served miserable, destitute and handicapped people and gave messages of love and kindness. He used to say that the mercy of God is more on the gentle and noble persons. Jesus used to say that you should know that the kingdom of God is within you. Gradually the popularity of Jesus grew. Having seen this, the conservative and the ruling elites became suspicious and they implicated Jesus in false case and hanged him on the cross. It is said that while dying, Jesus said, "Oh God! Forgive them, because they don't know what sin they are committing?" Christians believe that on the third day of death, Jesus Christ was resurrected and went to heaven. Christianity began to spread rapidly after the martyrdom of Jesus. Christian missionaries preached this religion vigorously and gradually it became the largest religion in the world.

There are many sects in Christianity, including Catholics, Protestants, Orthodox and Anglicans etc. By the sixteenth century, some clergies raised voices against the growing religious hypocrisy and political hegemony of the Pope and criticised the religious deviation in which John Wycliffe and Martin Luther were prominent. They criticized the view of the Pope and insisted on the reform in Christianity. Those who raised their voice for the reform in Christianity were called Protestants and gradually the Church of the Protestants was also separated. Christianity is divided into six main groups: The Church of the East, Oriental Orthodoxy, Eastern Orthodox, Roman Catholicism, Protestantism and Restorationism.

7
ISLAM RELIGION

Islam is the second largest religion in the world after Christianity in terms of population. It originated in Mecca, Saudi Arabia in the seventh century AD. Its founder was Prophet Muhammad ibn Abdullah al Hasheem, who was born in the Qureshi tribe of Mecca, the city of Saudi Arabia in the year 570 AD. A few days after his birth his father Abdullah died and his mother Amina died when Muhammad was only six years old. Orphan Muhammad was raised by his uncle Abtalib ibn and his wife Halima.

Muhammad's uncle used to trade by camels from Syria and Mohammed accompanied him from the age of fourteen. But Muhammad did not pay much attention to the business. He used to spend time in listening to the sermons of religious leaders. In those days, there were discourses of religious teachers of various religions at Kaaba of Mecca. The people of the neighbourhood considered Muhammad a man of religious instinct. At the age of about 25, his uncle got him married to a 40-year-old widow named Khadijah bint Khuwaylid who was financially wealthy. Now Muhammad began to spend more time in listening to the sermons of Christian and Jewish gurus. He sometime meditated in the hill caves of Mecca. It is believed that when Muhammad was 40 years old, one day he was sitting in meditation of God in a mountain cave called Hera, he saw the Gabriel i.e., the messenger of Allah in the cave. It is believed that the messenger of Allah conveyed the message of Allah to Muhammad. The believers of Islam believe this incident to be true, but the scholars of Judaism call this incident as fabricated and say that the incident of Gabriel coming to meet Muhammad is fabricated. Jewish believe that no other Messiah after Moses has yet been born in the Abrahamic religion. They say that there is still a big time left for the Messiah to be born.

However, after returning from the Cave of Hera Mountain, Muhammad told this incident to his wife Khadija. Khadija told this to some neighbours and relatives, but except a few people, other people did not believe in this story of Muhammad. On the contrary some people ridiculed him. But Muhammad did not heed to this criticism and started propagating his religion among the people but he did not get any success in his home place Mecca. On the contrary most of the Meccans started making fun of him. Then Muhammad with some of his supporters went to Medina, another Arab city. Muhammad's journey towards Medina is considered a historical event in Islam, as from this time the Hijri calendar begins.

On those days, there was a lot of infighting among the residents of medina which benefited Muhammad. Muhammad gained considerable support in Medina and formed an army of about ten thousand supporters and again stormed towards Mecca where the Meccans did not dare to oppose him and the Meccans surrendered before him. Some historians believe that Muhammad defeated the Meccans in the battle and his supporters looted and there was bloodshed in Mecca. Thus, Islam emerged as a religious cum political organization which later transformed into the Caliphate system. The Caliphate system was abolished in 1924 after the abolition of the Ottoman sultanate. Prior to this, the Ottoman sultan was ex officio caliph. Islam continued to be a religious cum political organization even after the death of Muhammad. Even today there is a mixture of religion and politics in almost all Islamic countries of the world, whereas religion is to show the path of understanding oneself and to connect oneself with God. What has religion to do with politics?

Islam means peace, but the key element of peace and non-violence is not visible in Islam. Non-violence, compassion and peace are considered to be the basic elements of religion which are not seen in Islam. The incident of Karbala ground and the killing of Imam Hasan ibn Ali and his companions are the evidence of this fact.

Muhammad propagated his religion for about 22 years. He died in the year 632 AD in Medina at the age of 62 years and he was buried in Medina. After the death of Mohammed some of his supporters wanted to make his nephew and son-in-law Ali ibn Abu Talib to be his heir but majority of people had chosen Abubaker, the father-in-law of Mohammed and the father of his youngest wife Ayasha as their first caliph and successor. The differences between the supporters of Ali ibn Abu Talib and Abubakar deepened and later it split into Shia and Sunni sects.

There are also some sub sects in Islam such as Ahmadiyya, Alawi, Druze, Hanafi, Ismaili, Jafari, Kharijites, Maliki, Shafi, Sufi, Wahabi, Zaidi, etc.

The main texts of Islam are the Quran and the Hadith. The following *five basic precepts has to be followed by every Muslim.*

1. *Reading Shahada (Declaration of Faith) - Every Muslim has to declare the supremacy of God and Muhammad as the Prophet of Islam. This declaration is called reading Kalema or Shahada. It is said that there is no God other than Allah and Muhammad is his messenger.*
2. *Performing Namaz (prayer) - Every Muslim should perform Namaz five times every day and on every Friday after two o'clock Namaz should be offered in the mosque.*
3. *Giving zakat - donating to poor and destitute people.*
4. *To keep fasting - To observe fasting during the holy month of Ramadan.*
5. *Hajj- Every Muslim should go to Hajj once in life according to his/her financial Capacity.*

8
RISE OF SUFISM

The impact of violence and bloodshed is apparent on Islam since its origin in Arab. The incidents of Karbala and the murder of Hazarat Ibn Ali Talib are glaring examples. There are many examples of violence, bigotry and intolerance towards other religions in Islam. Because of these negative aspects in Islam, the people of spiritual instinct felt uncomfortable from the beginning. Due to the conservative and intolerant policies of Islam, some saintly people wanted to bring love and generosity in Islam. This sentiment laid the backdrop of Sufism. Although the views of Sufis never received the support of the wider sections of Muslims. Even the Sufis had to face the onslaught of fundamentalism of Islam and many Sufi saints had to lose their lives.

First of all, Mansoor al-Allaz had to be martyred in 922 AD. Mansoor Al Allaz was a resident of Iran. He was a poet and one of the promoters of the Tasawwuf (Sufi) sect. He was declared anti-Islam and was tortured to death on the order of the Abbasid Caliph al-Muqtadar. He talked about the principles of Fana (Samadhi) Moksha and Nirvana like Indian religions. He said that Fana is the ultimate aim of human life.

Sufi saint and well-known Punjabi poet Bulleh Shah (Syed Abdullah Shah Qadri) says about the hypocrisy and ignorance spread in Islam –

Parh Parh Kitaaban Ilm Diyan Tu Naam Rakh Leya Qazi
Hath Vich Pharke Talwaar Tu Naam Rakh Leya Ghaazi

Makkay Madeena Ghum Aya Te Naam Rakh Leya Haaji
O Bulleya Haasil Ki Kitta? Je Tu Rab Na Kitta Raazi.'

Bulleh Shah has mocked the hypocrisy prevailing in Islam and states that by reading only books you became Qazi and by doing violence you became Gazi and after visiting Mecca and Medina you became Haji, but you have no knowledge about God.

The word 'Sufi' derives from the Arabic word 'saf' which means purity. Some people believe that Suf also means wool. Since the Sufi saint (dervesh) usually wore white wool clothes, this is why they were called Sufi. One thing is clear that Sufi saints disagree with the fundamentalist and orthodox views of Islam. However, these Sufis also had two categories which are called Basra and Besra. Basra believes in Islamic Sharia but Besras are those who do not believe in Islamic laws and are fully devoted to service of Allah. According to the orthodox rules of Islam, singing is considered un-Islamic, while Besra Sufi considers qawwali as a means to get mercy of Allah.

Sufism is believed to have originated in the city of Basra, Iraq, about a thousand years ago. Persons such as Rabia Basri, Ibrahim ibn Adham and Mansoor Al Hallaj are considered to be its founder. Thereafter poets like Abū Ḥamīd bin Abū Bakr Ibrahim popularly known as Attar, Jalal al-Din Muhammad Rumi and Hafez are counted in this category who wanted to spread love among people through their poetries. Sufi Saint Jalaluddin Rumi says through his poem that,

"The sun's rays fall on the wall and the wall starts shining but in reality, it is not its own radiance, similarly everything in this world has nothing of its own merit, so you must know the source, which always shines with its own light."

Main features of Sufism: -

1. *Sufism or Tasawwuf is the mystic sect of Islam. Sufi saints put emphasis on the internal purity, while orthodox Muslims emphasize on the external conduct and religious rituals.*

2. *Sufism believes that the realization of God is achieved through devotion. In order to attain God (Allah), it is necessary for the devotee to have love for God.*
3. *Sufism believes that love and devotion are the only way to reach to God.*
4. *In addition to Prophet Muhammad, Sufism has also given great importance to Murshid or Pir.*
5. *Sufism believes that devotion is more important than Roja (fasting) or Namaz.*
6. *Sufism emphasizes that there should not be any intermediary between God and devotees. Therefore, devotion is the means to attain God.*
7. *Going to Sufi Mazars is called Jiyarat. Particularly, the dancing and singing Qawwali are the parts of devotion. Sufi saints believe that singing (jīkra and Sama), chanting of the name of God is total devotion. Chishti Sama was popularized by Amir Khosrow.*

Ten steps of Sufism -

1. *Tooba - (Repentance) - Regrets for own past bad deeds or conduct.*
2. *Zuhad literally means piety (righteousness based on purity)*
3. *Vara - the practice of self-restraint.*
4. *Fakar - do not keep more money than the minimum requirement.*
5. *Sabra - patience and tolerance.*
6. *Shukar- Gratitude.*
7. *Raza - Being optimistic.*
8. *Riza – Complete surrender to Allah.*
9. *Khauf - Fear of evil or sinful action.*
10. *Tauvakkul - to be happy in any situation in life.*

Six ways to reach to God -

1. *Abudiyat - mental attitude of servitude or be slave of Allah.*
2. *Allahe Bandagi - Love for God and His creations.*
3. *Zohar – sanctity and control on own senses.*
4. *Marfat- Self-realization means that I am not a body but the soul.*

5. *Hakiqat – Self-realisation or union with God.*
6. *Wajd – Wajd or wajad is term used for the religious ecstasy induced by dhikr (the remembrance of God) by means of Sama, listening to the measured recitation, singing or chanting of spiritual verses or poetry.*

Methods of meditation in Sufism -

1. *Habse Vassar – Concentration by closing the eyes.*
2. *Habse Dum - Breathing Exercise i.e., Pranayama.*
3. *Shamma - Listening the Kirtan of God.*
4. *Istejat - to recite the name of God in the heart.*
5. *Sagale Sarmadi - remembrance of God in mind.*

The main sects of Sufism

The renowned historian Abul Fazal has mentioned fourteen Sufi sects in the 'Aaine Akbari', but in India, the Chishti, Suhrawardy, Kadiri, Firdausi, Naqshbandi and Satir sects have been predominantly influential.

The saints of Chishti sect lived in their khanqahs (monasteries) and lived a simple life, keeping a distance from sultans and emperors. They avoided politics and used to be engaged day and night in the service of Allah. They were indifferent to the world's hypocrisy and remained detached from the world, but Suhrawardy Sufi used to stay close to the sultans and Nawabs and took government donations. The saints of Chishti Silsila did not follow the Islamic religious laws and like Hindu, Jain and Buddhist saints and Monks lived in penance and meditation and were detached from worldly pleasures. The Sufis of Naqshbandi sect followed the rules of Islam. In this way, Chishti Sufi saints were like the saints of the Bhakti movement of India and were engaged in devotion to God. This is why Chishti Sufis were respected among Hindus too.

Chishti sect of Sufism started in Persia (Iran) and its founder was Abu Abdal Chishti but in India Chishti sect was started by Khawaja

Moinuddin Chishti. Moinuddin Chishti was born in Iran. He was a fakir since childhood and became a disciple of Khawaja Osman Hasan. Khawaja Moinuddin Chishti came to India in 1190 and got built his khanqah (monastery) in Ajmer. Even today, during his death anniversary, Ursa fair is held at his tomb. Ursa means submerging in God.

Khawaja Moinuddin Chishti had two famous disciples named Sheikh Hamimuddin Nagauri and Qutubuddin Bakhtiar. Qutbuddin Bakhtiyar got built his Khanqah (ashram) in Delhi. Qutbuddin Bakhtiyar's disciple was Baba Sheikh Farid whose views influenced Guru Nanak and his verses have also been compiled in Guru Granth Saheb. Baba Sheikh Farid's disciple was Sheikh Nizamuddin Auliya, who was born in Badaun, Uttar Pradesh, who gave a message of quietness and tolerance. People of all religions respected him. Since Chishti saints were not bound by Islamic rules and emphasized on the unity of all religions, they were respected among the people of all religions. The Chishti Sufi saints did not deal with the Sultans and avoided politics. Sheikh Nizamuddin Auliya's disciple was Sheikh Salim Chishti who got built his khanqah at Fatehpur Sikri. Emperor Akbar had high respect for Salim Chishti.

9
THE TRUE MEANING OF DHARMA AND ITS CHARACTERISTICS

Eighty percent of the people of the world believe in some religion, creed, sect or any other supernatural power. Only 20 percent of the people do not believe in any religion and they are either atheists or agnostics. China has the largest number of atheists. The rise of communism under the leadership of Mao in China obliterated archaic cultural system along with moral or spiritual views of Confucian and Lao Tzu. China is an economically prosperous nation but spiritually and morally backward.

Generally, people understand the meaning of religion as faith in some supernatural powers and its associated customs, traditions, method of worship and religious views. The meaning of religion is generally deemed as prevalent cultural system. Each religion has its own practice, rituals, sacred texts, holy places, codes of conduct, deities, temples, mythological stories and organisations. Religious practices are the system of rituals, sermons, prayers, sacrifices, festivals, celebrations, marriages, process of carcass immersion, music, art, dance, public service or other aspects of human culture or the history and stories of religions which are preserved in their sacred texts, symbols or places.

People in this world are divided into theist and atheist without knowing the truth. In fact, both theists and atheists are living in delusion because they have only belief, not research. Religion is based on faith and there is no rationale for belief.

There are an estimated ten thousand religions in the world, but in terms of population of the world, 75 percent of the people are associated with four religions namely, Christian, Islam, Hindu and Buddhism. The Christianity and Islam originated in the Arab countries of West Asia whereas Hinduism and Buddhism originated in India.

Although every religion claims that the purpose of religion is to give meaning to the human life by showing the right path, but history is witness to the fact that innumerable battles, crusades, violence, hatred, atrocities and terrorism have occurred due to communal confrontation in the world. Some people believe that some religions have brainwashed the people and made them ignorant. Religion and creed have created hatred in the people by creating differences among the human beings, due to this, confrontation frequently happens. Many religions have tried to convert people of other religions by fear, force or inducement. Some communal organizations have fooled people in the name of God. Many sects have spread many kinds of evils, superstitions, hypocrisy and kept the people in ignorance. The gurus, priests, mullahs and clerics of some religions misused the religion. In the medieval period, there have been many incidents of cheating, fraud of grabbing the wealth of innocent people by making false claims of sending them to heaven. Some religions have said unscientific facts and even gave death sentence to some scientists. Torturing of Galileo is an example of this fact. However, the nature treats every man, animal and plant equally. Nature gives air, water and sunlight to all so that all may live, but some selfish and cunning people deliberately created discrimination and hatred among human beings and pushed them in ignorance. Religion was resorted to carry out this nefarious design and people were enslaved under the guise of religion or sect. In Hinduism, on the basis of Manu Samhita, vertical Varnashrama was created and the Shudras (Dalits) standing at the bottom layer were exploited for many centuries under the guise of religion. They were treated like slaves and untouchables for centuries. Even on the basis of Manu Smriti, women too were treated unequally. Not only in Hinduism, but also in Christianity and Islam, the slave system continued for centuries.

In Islam, women were treated inferior not only on the basis of burqa but also for many other reasons. Thus, religion has been misused for centuries. With the developing of awareness, the people are losing faith in many religions. The foundation of some religions depends on the ignorance of people and they do not want free inquiry and awakening among the people.

The right religion is that by which one can find the right path of life. If religion is not for the welfare of all, then it cannot be called religion and should not be followed. Religion is that which can be adopted - 'Dhri' Dharayati iti dharma.' In this way only the noble values such as purity, peace, non-violence, truth, honesty, morality, virtue, justice, cleanliness, love, compassion, friendliness and gratitude have been called religion since ancient times. In the absence of the above qualities, human life will collapse. Actually, dharma enjoins a sense of duty, just as purity of mind is necessary for peace and bliss. If mind is dirty or polluted, it will remain restless and will produce pain. Therefore, it is the religion of every person to keep his/her mind clean so that he/she remains happy and also make other beings happy through noble deeds.

Gautama Rishi, the pioneer of Nyaya Darshan, said that-

> 'Yato Abhyudyanishrayas Siddhi: Sah Dharma.' Means the action through which one gets progress and happiness is the religion.

Dharma is universal. It is eternal, unchanging beyond the time, boundary and community. The heat and light are the inherent qualities of fire and the coolness is the inherent quality of ice. These inherent qualities of fire and ice never change. Similarly, there are some basic elements of human life without which human life is meaningless, for example every man wants happiness and peace in his life. How human beings can get peace and bliss in life has been told by ancient rishis and yogis of India.

The word Dharma has been used many times in the Rigveda, but the term began to be used mostly during the reign of Emperor

Ashoka. In the scriptures, social duties have also been considered dharma such as son dharma, father dharma, wife dharma, raj dharma, ashram dharma, guru dharma, disciple dharma etc.

Definition of Dharma according to **Manu-**

'Dhriti: Kshama Damosteyeyam Shouchmindriyanigraha'.
Dhirvidya Satyamakrodho Dasakah Dharmalakshanam. (Manusmriti- 6.92)

Meaning - Manu has enumerated the ten signs of dharma: - dhriti (patience), kshama (forgiveness), dum (always engaged in dharma with restraint), asteya (not stealing), sauch (cleanness of body and mind), indriyanigraha (controlling the senses and mind and engaged in righteousness), dhir (enhancing the intellect with virtuous deed), vidya (taking real knowledge). Satyam (always speak truth) and Akrodha (be calm).

Dharma according to **Padma Purana** -

'Shrooyataam dharmasarvasvam shrutvaa chaiva vichaaryataam
Aatmanah pratikoolaani paresha na samaacharet.'
(Padmapuran, Shrishti- 19 / 357-358)

(Meaning: What is the essence of religion? Listen it and follow it and don't behave with other person in a way which is unbecoming to yourself.

According to the ancient jurist **Yajnavalkya**, there are nine characteristics of religion:

'Ahimsa Satyamastayam Shouchmindriyanigraha:.
Danam Damo Daya Shanti: Sarveshan Dharmasadhnam'.
(Yajnavalkya Smriti- 1.122)

(Non-violence, truth, non-stealing (asteya), cleanliness, senses control (subdue the senses), charity, restraint (dum), kindness and peace are the sign of dharma)

Dharma according to **Vatsyyana,**

Vatsyyana has clarified dharma by comparing with adharma (unrighteousness). Vatsyyana believes that the religion is related to the mind, speech and action, (mansa, vacha and karma). In other words, religion should be observed by thought, speech and action.

Dharma of the body – Dana, Paritran and paricharan means charity, welfare of self and service to others.

The Adharma of the body - violence, asteya (stealing), indulging in prohibited sex.

The dharma of speech and writing - truth, pious speech and self-inspection.

Adharma of speech and writing – false, hateful and harmful speech and expression.

Dharma of mind - Mercy, detachment and reverence to God.

Adharma of the mind - envy, greed and atheism.

In **Bhagavata Purana** thirty characteristics of religion have been enumerated-

'Satya Daya Tapa: Shaucham Titiksha Shamo Dum:
Ahimsa Brahmacharya tyag: Swadhyaya Arjavam.
Santosh: Samdrikah Seva Gramyehopram: Shanai:
Nrinam viparyayeheksha mounamatvimarshanam.
Annadhyade samvibhago Bhutebhayascha yatharhathh.
Teshtāmadevatabuddhi: Sutarana Nrishu Pandava.
Shravanam Kirtanam Chasya Smaranam Mahtam Gate:
Svejyavanatirdasya sakhyamatamasamardanam.
Nrnamayam paro dharma: sarvesha samudayhritah.
Trishulakshanwan Rajan Sarvatma Yen Tushyati.'

That is, truth, kindness, penance, purity, forbearance (the state of mind in which one bears the pain inflicted by others and there is no sense of revenge for it), knowing difference between just and unfair, restraint of mind, sense of sobriety, non-violence, celibacy, renunciation, self-study or self-analysis, simplicity, contentment, insight, service to saints, gradual retirement from worldly pleasures, the reversal of pride, silence and self-inspection are the thirty characteristics of dharma.

Mahabharata talks about dharma that-

'Dharmah satam hitah punsam dharmascaivasrah satam
Dharmallokastrayastata pravrittah scharachrah.'

That is, dharma is in the interest of the right persons. Dharma is the shelter of right persons and the all three worlds or loka (Realms) namely, heaven, earth and space are ruled by dharma, i.e., the entire universe is controlled by the rules of dharma, i.e., natural laws.

According to **Goswami Tulsi Das** –

'Parhit saris dharm nahi bhai par peeda sam nahi adhmai.'

That is, welfare of others is best religion and hurting others is the biggest sin.

In **Ramcharit Manas**, Goswami Tulsi Das writes -

'Sunhu sakha, Kah Kripanidhana, Jehin jai hoi so syandan aana.
Sauraj Dhiraj Tehi Ratha Chaka, Satya Sheel drirhha dhwaja pataka.
Bal Bibek Dum Par-Hita Ghore, Chhama Kripa Samata Raju Jore.
Ish Bhajanu sarathi Sujana, Birati Charm Santosh Kripaana.
Dan parsu budhi sakti prachanda, bar bigyan kathhin kodanda.
Amal Achal Man Tron Samana, Sama Jam Niyam Silimukh Nana.
Kavach Abhed Bipra-Gurupuja, ehi sam bijay upaya Na dooja.
Sakha Dharmayam Aas ratha, jake, jitan kahah n katahu ripu take.

Maha Ajay Sansar Ripu, Jiti Sakai So Bir.
Jaake as rath hoi drirhha, sunhu sakha mati-dheer.'

Goswami Tulsi Das writes in the Lanka kand (chapter) of Ramacharit Manas that Vibhishana saw Ravana on the chariot in the battle field and Rama without chariot. Having seen shri Rama without chariot, Vibhishana became impatient and began to doubt on the success of shri Rama in good faith and love for Rama. Having seen the frustration of Vibhishana, Shri Ram told his friend that "oh friend Vibhishana! Listen to me - the chariot that brings victory is another one."

The courage and patience are the wheels of that chariot. Truth and good conducts (virtue) are his strong flag. Strength, wisdom, subjugation of the senses and philanthropy are four horses who are connected to the chariot with forgiveness, mercy and equanimity. The hymn of God is the clever charioteer driving that chariot. Vairagya (detachment) is a shield, contentment is sword, charity is a tomahawk, wisdom is a strong power, excellence in science is bow, a pure (orderly) and stable mind is like a Quiver, sham (subdue the mind), the non-violence -truth – Asteya (non- stealing) - celibacy - Aparigraha (non -possession of excessive wealth) are yama and purity- containment, penance, self- introspection and God-pursuit are the niyama. Worship of learned people and gurus are the armours. There is no other way of victory without having the aforesaid dharma qualities.

'Oh friend! There are no enemies to win for those who have such a religion. Oh friend! Kindly listen to me with patience and wisdom - a hero who has such a strong chariot can also conquer a big formidable enemy like this samsara (cycle of birth and death) and what to talk of this small enemy, Ravana?'

In fact, in ancient India, Dharma was the code of conduct for the purity in life. It was a pious duty and not hypocrisy, custom or rituals as prevailing today. The rituals are said to be the ignorance and impediment in the way of liberation. That is why it was said that 'Yato Dharma: Tato Jai' means where there is dharma, there is victory.

SECOND CHAPTER - YOGA

10
ORIGIN OF YOGA

'Yoga' is a Sanskrit word and its meaning is to connect. It is a mental and spiritual process to connect oneself with one's soul (consciousness) or God. This mental and spiritual process makes the mind calm, restrained, intelligent and joyful and removes ignorance. It leads oneself from darkness to the light i.e., from ignorance to enlightenment. This is the ancient education of India. Today the whole world knows about yoga. Every year on 21st June, 'World Yoga Day' is celebrated on the directive of the United Nations. Looking at the antiquity of yoga, it is believed that its originator is Yogeshwar Maheshwar Shiva, whose idols are found in meditation posture. The idol of Mahadev Shiva reflects the entire Yoga philosophy.

Lord Shiva is considered to be the greatest yogi in Hindu philosophy, who keeps on doing welfare to all creatures while remaining detached from the Maya of this world. Statues of Shiva are depicted in meditative posture sitting on the deer skin in the background of the white Himalayas, under the blue sky. Shiva is shown wrapped with charred ashes and snake as garland in his neck. Ganga is emanating from the matted hair. Apart from the 'third eye' and blue neck, the trident, pellet drum (Damaru) are shown in one hand and an oblong water pot (Kamandala) is shown in the other hand. The parallel sandal mark 'tripund Chandan' is shown on the forehead of Lord Shiva.

In the middle of Parallel sandal mark (Tripund Chandan) the 'third eye' is depicted which means - the inner vision emanating from the soul, that is, uplifting one-self above sato, rajo and tamo gunas through the right vision and forgetting the worries of past and future and to remain in present. Opening of the third eye signifies the disappearance of ignorance. Shiva sitting in meditative posture with open eyes signify that a person should remain calm and restrained in the day-to-day business like a yogi.

Sitting on the deer skin means that one should suppress the fickleness of the mind and senses, that is, the mind and senses must be kept under the control. The snake in the neck has two meanings - always keep the rope of yoga tied to the neck and keep on meditating. The mouth of the snake wrapped in the neck of Shiva hangs down, which means keeping the ego under the control of the soul.

Blue neck (Neelkanth) means the negative feelings or thoughts. It is neither to be expressed outside nor be taken to the heart, but it should be modified by wisdom. A person should be a yogi like Shiva and the worldly negativity (poisons) should not be allowed to pollute the mind. That is, we should make a habit of avoiding negative thoughts.

The matted hair of Shiva is a symbol of wisdom derived through meditation. The Ganges is a symbol of purity and coolness and the moon of second moonlit night on the forehead is a symbol of peace. All these signify that when the mind remains cool and clean, then there will be awareness of wisdom and happiness in the mind.

The ashes of corpse on Shiva's body reminds that everything in this world is transient and perishable. This beautiful physique, wealth and fame are all temporary, only God is the truth and one should be curious to know him and remain detached from the illusion and negativity of this world.

The trident in one hand symbolizes three types of sorrows. 'Shul' means sorrows which are of three types i.e., bodily, economic and divine. All these three sorrows change from time to time. Therefore, one should not lose patience. Keep the mind restrained and apply wisdom in the time of bad days. Shiva's kamandala is a symbol of detachment of mind and senses from outer negativity and ignorance. The blue sky is the symbol of the vastness of universe. The white

Himalayas symbolises the purity of life. Thus, the image of Shiva is sufficient to explain the philosophy of yoga.

During the excavation of Mohenjo-Daro and Harappa in the Indus Valley, the bronze seals of Shiva in the yogi posture have been found. It is of around three to four thousand BC. This shows that yoga is too old and it is also called Pashupata or Maheshwara Yoga.

The Bhagavad Gita gives a detailed account of yoga. Lord Krishna imparted education of the various dimensions of yoga to his disciple Arjuna, in which Samkhya or jnana, Bhakti (devotion) and Karma Yoga have been explained. In addition to Upanishads, there is also mention of Yoga in Jain and Buddhist literature. In this way, yoga education has been coming since the beginning, but the credit goes to Maharishi Patanjali for collecting yoga knowledge. Maharishi Patanjali's Yoga philosophy or Yoga Sutra is an important part of Indian shad Darshana, (six philosophies). Many things mentioned in the Yoga Sutras of Maharishi Patanjali are also mentioned in the Samkhya philosophy of Maharishi Kapil. The Samkhya philosophy of Maharishi Kapil is considered to be the foundation of Indian philosophy, because many things of Samkhya philosophy have been repeated in numerous other Indian philosophies apart from Bhagavad Gita.

There are 195 sutras in Maharishi Patanjali's Yoga sutra which are divided into four parts or chapters i.e. Samadhi Pada (51 Sutras), Sadhana Pada(55 Sutras), Vibhuti Pada(55 sutras) and Kaivalya Pada(34 Sutras). The purpose of yoga and the symptoms of mind disorders has been described in the Samadhi Pada. In the sadhana pada, mental pain and effect of karma, etc. have been discussed and means have been given to remove mental variations. Vibhutipada describes the achievements of yoga and meditation, i.e., the attainment of siddhis. In the Kaivalya pada there is description about complete destruction of the sadhaka's ignorance, the end of attachment and malice and the attainment of 'Kaivalya' i.e., salvation. After attaining Kaivalya, the sadhaka gets freedom from the cycle of birth and death. Actually, Kaivalya means attainment of salvation which is the ultimate goal of yoga.

Apart from the Yoga Sutras of Maharishi Patanjali, Hatha Yoga Pradipika is a famous book related to Hatha Yoga. It is in Sanskrit and Guru Gorakhnath is considered to be its author. There are also two other famous texts on Hatha Yoga namely, Gherand Samhita and Shiva Samhita. The Shiva Samhita describes Yoga through dialogue between Lord Shiva and Goddess Parvati. This book was composed in the 15th century. Matsyendra natha, a 10th century yogi who was revered in both Buddhist and Hindu traditions is traditionally considered the revivalist of hatha yoga as well as the author of some of its earliest texts. He is also considered as the founder of the 'natha sect' and guru of Goraknath. In Hatha yoga 'H' stands for the Sun and 'Th' stands for the moon. There are several thousand arteries and veins (nadis) in the human body, among them there are three major nadis i.e., the Sun (Suryanadi) also called 'Pingala' which passes through the right nostril. Moon (Chandranadi) or 'Eda' which passes through the hole of the left nostril. The third pulse is 'Sushumna' between these two vessels in the spinal cord. Thus, Hatha Yoga is the process in which the 'Prana Vayu' is made to enter into the Sushumna Nadi with the help of the Pingala and Eda nadi.

The Hatha Pradipika describes the four parts of Hatha Yoga - Asana, Pranayama, Mudra, Bandh and nadanusandhan. Gheranda Samhita describes the seven limbs - hetkarma, asana, mudrabandha, pranayama, meditation, samadhi etc.

There are mainly four types of yoga namely, Gyan Yoga, Bhakti Yoga, Karma Yoga and Raja Yoga. The only purpose of these four yoga is to associate oneself with the soul and God and to dispel ignorance, because 'avidya' (Ignorance) is the cause of human suffering. If avidya is ousted, then the problem of suffering and happiness ends and the state of equanimity is gained. Lord Shri Krishna explained the meaning of the 'state of equanimity' to Arjuna that when mind remains detached from pain and pleasure, love and hate, victory and defeat, gain and loss, it is said to be in the state of equanimity. (Bhagavad Gita-2/56)

Maharishi Patanjali considers yoga to be the means for removal of defilement from Chita or regulation of the Chita, whereas in the Bhagavad Gita, Shri Krishna describes Yoga to be the evenness in every situation in the duality of sorrow - happiness, gain - loss, victory – defeat, cold -hot, enmity - friendship. 'Siddhyasiddhyo: Samo Bhootva Samatvam Yoga Uchhyate', (Bhagavad Gita-2/48)

Again, Shri Krishna says that, there should be no bondage of karma in performing duty. Therefore, the duty should be performed without any attachment. 'Yoga Karmasu kaushalam', (Bhagavad Gita-2/50). According to Buddhism, 'Kushal Chittakaggata Yoga' means-the skill of concentration of mind is yoga.

The regular practice of asanas, pranayama and meditation awaken consciousness and transmit cosmic energy into the body and keep the mind calm and joyful. Removal of negative emotions such as sexual desire, anger, greed, violence and hatred from the mind and cultivating positive emotions like non-violence, kindness, love and benevolence is the aim of yoga.

The story of 'Samudra Manthan' [the Churning of the Ocean] appears in two puranas namely, Bhagavad Purana and Vishnu Purana, as well as in the Mahabharata. The story of Samudra Manthan goes like this. Once upon a time, due to the curse of Durvasa Rishi, Devraj Indra became powerless because he was dethroned from all three lokas, namely deva loka, bhoo loka and patala loka. The king Bali, (the king of demons) became the master of all the three worlds. Indra and other devas had lost their power which made them dejected. Indra under the leadership of Brahma went to Vaikuntha to meet Lord Vishnu. Brahma narrated the predicament of devas before Lord Vishnu and pleaded for his help. Then Lord Vishnu advised Indra and other devas that in this time of crisis, it is better for them to forget hostility with demons and try to have a treaty with them in order to recover their lost power. Lord Vishnu advised Indra for the joint venture of devas and the demons for churning of the ocean. Lord Vishnu further said that this venture will yield many valuable wealth as well as nectar. After this venture all devas will again become powerful.

On the advice of Lord Vishnu, Devraj Indra went to meet King

Bali and spoke to him lovingly and proposed the plan of Samudra Manthan and talked about starting a joint effort to make it successful. King Bali accepted the proposal of Indra. With the combined power of devas and demons, the plan of churning of the ocean began. The 'Basuki Nag' was made the rope from the top of the Mount Mandhara. Devas were on the one side of the rope and the demons were on the other side. Meanwhile, Lord Vishnu became a giant tortoise (Kurm) to support the Mandhara Mountain and sat at the bottom of the mountain.

The work of the churning of the sea started with the combined force of devas and demons. In the beginning a deadly poison called halahal was found. Everyone got frightened by 'halahal' and its shocking effects. Then Lord Shiva Shambhu, the incarnation of compassion, consumed the halahal poison in order to mitigate worries of all and kept the poison in his throat, due to which his throat became blue. Since then, he is called 'Neelkanth Mahadeva'.

From the churning of the sea many valuable gems and other items were found. Devas and the demons shared the items recovered from the churning of the ocean. In the end, when the urn of nectar was found from the churning of the ocean, the demons grabbed the nectar. Then Lord Vishnu turned himself into a very beautiful young woman called Mohini in order to lure the demons. Having seen Mohini, the demons got enchanted. The Mohini took the urn of nectar from the demons and gave it to devas. When the demons, named Rahu and Ketu, understood this trick of Lord Vishnu, they changed their attire and tried to drink nectar by joining the line of devas, then Sun God revealed about the identity of those two demons to Lord Vishnu. Thereafter Lord Vishnu separated the heads of Rahu and Ketu from their bodies by Sudarshan Chakra.

The story of Samudra Manthan is depicted through painting at the third gate of the world-famous giant Angkor temple in northern Cambodia.

In fact, there is a symbolic meaning behind every archaic Indian mythology. Actually, the story has been written to explain the secret of spirituality and yoga through symbols and stories. The secret of meditation is hidden behind this story of Samudra Manthan.

This whole story explains that, as a tortoise withdraws its mouth inside its strong shell, similarly a practitioner of meditation must sit in the meditation posture by withdrawing his mind and senses from outside. The stream of endless tides of thoughts in mind (Mandhar), should be tied to the rope of yoga and churning the ocean inside own self with the combined effort of positive and negative energy should be started. In the beginning some distress or pain (halalal, venom) will arise which should be tolerated like Lord Shiva. Gradually, through continuous yoga practice one will receive many things which will be priceless, pleasant and enjoyable like nectar. All these things will bring amazing changes in life. But do not be fascinated by those divine gifts, but lead life like a yogi with detachment, because attachment is the root cause of bondage and ignorance, which leads to sufferings.

11
JNANA (GYAN) YOGA

The word 'Avidya' (Ignorance) has been used many times in the Yoga Sutras of Maharishi Patanjali, Upanishads, Buddhism and Jain literatures. Avidya is considered the biggest barrier to the enlightenment and salvation. The ignorance about 'Brahma' and the 'soul' are considered avidya by Upanishads but avidya has a wide meaning. Not knowing the difference between proper and improper, the lack of mental ability of reasoning and analysis, ignorance about the nature and its eternal rules such as its variability, impermanence and perishable qualities, lack of knowledge about the nature of mind, the state of unawareness about the consciousness, are called 'avidya'. One cannot understand the difference between truth, illusion and falsehood due to ignorance. Sexual desire, anger, greed, arrogance, attachment and envy darken the mind and create avidya.

While teaching Jnana Yoga to Arjuna, Lord Krishna says – 'wisdom is covered due to the craving, just as flame is covered by the smoke, the mirror by dirt and the embryo by the amnion.' (Bhagavat Gita- 3/38).

In fact, 'self-knowledge' is a state of 'self-realization', realization of atman or supreme consciousness. After self- knowledge the veil of ignorance is removed from the mind in the same way as darkness disappears after sunrise and life becomes illuminated and everything is clearly visible.

Saint Kabir says -

'Aatam anubhav jab bhayo, tab nhi harsh Vishad
Chitra deep sam habe rahe, taji kari bad-Vivad'.

When the experience of self-realization comes, the feeling of pleasure or pain goes away and it is settled like a picture of lamp, the debate on this topic is stopped.

Goswami Tulsi Das says -

'Gyan maan jaha ekhu nahi, dekh brahm saman sab mahi.' That is, when real knowledge comes, ego disappears from the mind and the person starts seeing the same 'Brahman' in all beings.

Baba Gorakhnath, the saint of the Nath sect says -

'Gyan Sarikha guru n miliya, chitt Sarika chella
Man Sarikha mail na miliya kaithe Gorakhnath Firey akela.'

Baba Gorakhnath says that knowledge is the greatest guru and quiet chitt is the greatest servant. Mind is a repository of filth. That is why Gorakhnath keeps his mind separate from the 'self'.

Lord Buddha said that man suffers in this world because of ignorance. The craving, attachment, ego and other emotional factors arise due to avidya (ignorance). He told his disciples that the mind is the source of ignorance. Therefore, we should watch our mind as a witness. Look at the mood of the mind and the feelings arising therein with the Vipassana meditation and find out its solution through wisdom. There are many types of disorders in the mind that keep changing the mood of a person, due to which restlessness, dissatisfaction and grief arise in the mind and wisdom starts disappearing. Just as everything appears clean in clear water, similarly if the mind is pure then life vision becomes clear. Therefore, Lord Buddha used to emphasize on the cleanness of the mind through meditation. Purity of mind is the first condition of Jnana yoga.

Once Lord Buddha was going somewhere with his disciples. On the way, he saw that a large number of animals were being taken to the king's palace by some people. Lord Buddha asked them, 'where are you taking these animals? Then the servants of the king replied that the animals are being taken to the palace to be sacrificed in the yajna. They told Lord Buddha that the priests have suggested the king to perform a yajna to attain heaven. Since the Vedic period, the practice of offering animal sacrifices was very common during yagnas.

After this, Lord Buddha went to the palace and said to the king – 'Oh king! If you can get heaven by sacrificing these animals, then it would be better to sacrifice me rather than sacrificing them. In this way you can definitely get heaven'. In those days the fame of Lord Buddha had spread in all directions. The king was forced to think after hearing his words. Buddha told the king, 'let us go to the pond in front of your palace.' Buddha told the king, that he should throw two earthen pots in the pond, one with rocks & stones and the other pot with ghee. Obeying Buddha, the king did the same. After a while, the rock-stone-filled pot sank to the bottom of the water, but the ghee of other pot started floating over the water. After this, Buddha said that – 'Oh king! - The rocks & stones are like your evil deeds. They sank to the bottom of the pond, but ghee is like your good deeds floating on the water. If you have desire to attain heaven then you should always do-good deeds. Good deeds will lift you up, but bad deeds are like rock-stones which will not let you get lifted but it will lead you to downfall. It is a sin to kill innocent animals. It can never lead you to heaven.'

Hearing the advice of Lord Buddha, the king realized his ignorance and bowed down at the feet of Lord Buddha. He apologized for his ignorance and gave up the idea of sacrificing animals.

Lord Krishna has said in the Bhagavad Gita that sexual desires, anger and greed – are the gates of hell and it brings about the ruination of soul. Therefore, one should avoid them. (Bhagavad Gita - 16/21)

The end of ignorance is possible only by knowledge. As the light of the sun drives away darkness, similarly the knowledge dispels ignorance. There are two types of knowledge- 'Apara Vidya' which is inferior knowledge and it is received by the senses, such as the knowledge gained from reading or listening to the scriptures. The knowledge that comes from reading and listening are inferior type of knowledge. This is not our own true knowledge but it is borrowed knowledge from someone else's experiences written in books. Such knowledge can only become our own after thorough examining it by our own experience or by meditation or by checking its truth. This method is called nididhyasana. Bookish knowledge can be adopted only after Nididhyasana.

'Para Vidya' is considered higher form of knowledge which is obtained through meditation or contemplation of mystic spiritual experience. According to the Mandukya Upanishad, this world is made up of three layers- first - the gross world which is experienced in the awaken state or Vaishvanara through the mind and the senses. In this awaken state, the cognitive senses gather worldly experience. One cannot know anything about God or consciousness in Vaishvanara state. The second state is the dream state in sleep in which the subtle world is experienced, and the third is the turya state, which is the state of samadhi. In the state of turiya or samadhi one gets experience of consciousness or God. In fact, this is the true awaken state wherein one gets higher knowledge. Such a knowledgeable person performs physical activities just like ordinary people, but his consciousness becomes divine. A person who has reached this state is able to see and understand the true nature of consciousness. The means to reach this state is the practice of continuous meditation. Apart from this, understanding the difference between the eternal and ephemeral, knowledge of conscience, the renunciation of worldly and heavenly desires is required. Observance of Sham, Dum, Shraddha, Samadhan, Uparti (detachment from worldly sensual pleasures), Titiksha (the power to bear sufferings) is required. That is six virtues, namely, evenness of mind, mastery over senses, observance of Dharma, endurance in tough conditions, faith in God, focus of mind and striving for the attainment of freedom from the cycle of birth and death i.e., salvation) are required to reach the state of enlightenment.

The worldly knowledge or the knowledge of scriptures cannot make a man enlightened. Self-knowledge is the experience of one's own self. Man gets wisdom through self-experience. Even after reading the scriptures a man behaves like an ignorant person. Sometimes the knowledge of scripture also creates false pride of knowledge which is basically avidya.

Once Kak Bhusundi had a desire to know about a person in this world who is considered to be ignorant even after becoming the scholar of all scriptures. He set out to find out such a person. After searching in the villages, in the cities and caves, he discovered that there was a Brahmin named Vidyadhar who was a scholar of the Vedas and Puranas and verses of several other scriptures were memorized by him. Kak Bhusundi was very happy to see a great scholar like Vidyadhar, but he was surprised that despite being such a scholar, people didn't consider him knowledgeable.

In order to find out why people do not consider Pandit Vidyadhar to be knowledgeable, Kak Bhusundi started following Pandit Vidyadhar to find out the truth. One day Pandit Vidyadhar was walking on the Nilgiri Mountain to enjoy the Van Vihara. At the same time while walking on the mountain, the princess of Kavand kingdom appeared before Pandit Vidyadhar. Seeing the beauty of the princess, Pandit Vidyadhar became lustful and forgot the pure beauty of nature. He got caught in the fascination of the physical beauty of the woman like a lustful animal. At that time neither he had knowledge of scriptures nor attention to the moral values. Even after being ignored by the princess, he did not realize and followed the princess. In the end, the princess's bodyguards caught him and put him in a prison.

Kak Bhusundi met Pandit Vidyadhar who was in jail. He said, 'oh so-called scholar! Could you not understand after reading so many scriptures that attachment is the cause of ignorance? Had you not been blind in the bodily attraction of the princess you would not have such a predicament.'

It has been said in the Vishnu Purana that,

'Tatkarma yanna bandhāya sā vidyā yā vimuktaye.
Āyāsāyāparaṃ karma vidyā'nyā śilpanaipuṇam.'

That is, the action is that which does not put in bondage – Vidya is that which liberates. That is, the action by which a man is not bound in bondage is the true Karma. That which leads to liberation is true knowledge. Bookish knowledge is avidya, real knowledge is that which is attained by intuition and liberation is attained only by vidya attained by meditation. The rest of the karma becomes the cause of bondage, due to which one often gets anxiety and pain.

It is necessary for the practitioners of Jnana Yoga to read, listen, contemplate and meditate on the sayings of great saints and sacred texts. Do independent analysis of its merits and demerits, just as husk and wheat are separated. Meditate on it (Nidhidhyasana) then there will be realization of its truth. Ghee is released only after churning the curd. Realization of the ultimate truth will happen only when there will be continuous cultivation and examination, otherwise there will be no benefit from mere bookish knowledge.

Sufi saint and famous Punjabi poet Baba Bulleh Shah says

'Padh Padh Ilm Hazaar Kitaaban
Kadi apne aap nu Padhya Nahin
Jaa jaa Wardey Mandar Masjid
Kadi Mann Apne wich padaya Nahin
Ainvein ladhda hai Shaitaan de Naal Bandeya
Kadi Nafs Apne Naal Larya Nahin
Aakhe Pir Bulleh Shah Aasmani Pharna Hain
Jehra Man wich wasda Unnhoo Phadya Nahin'

That is, you must have read thousands of books,
But you didn't try to read yourself.
You go to your temples and your mosques,

But you never tried to peep inside the self.
All your battles are with the vain devil,
But you never tried to fight the devil inside you.

12
BHAKTI (DEVOTION) YOGA

When a devotee realizes that he is nothing but his existence is on the mercy of God, he finally submerges in God and becomes united with the Almighty. This stage falls in the category of Bhakti Yoga.

Saint Kabir says -

'Jab mai tha to hari nahi,ab hari hai to main nahi
Prem gali ati sankari jame do na samahi.'

Meaning- when I was present there, there was no God, now I am not present, God is present there. The lane of love is very narrow wherein both cannot go together.

The gist of above couplet is that the path to reach to the God is very narrow. Only one can go through that path at a time. If you go alone, God will not be there. Therefore, you dissolve yourself in the Lord, then you will reach to the Lord, otherwise, you will be caught in a dilemma.

Where mind and the five senses are absent, that is, in the state of emptiness of samadhi, owns existence disappears and in that state, the ecstasy is realized. Where there is no sense of 'I', there is God.

Bhakti yoga is a state of total surrender before the God, unflinching love and unity with God. God is everything for the devotee. God is the master of the devotee and the devotee is the servant of God. For this reason, saints of the Bhakti period used to keep the title of 'das', (servant of God).

In the poem of Saint Ravidas, the sense of love and servitude to the Lord is reflected.

'Prabhuji, Tum Chandan, Hum Pani
Jaaki Ang Ang Baas Samaani
Prabhuji, Tum Ghan, Ban Hum Mora
Jaise Chitwat Chand Chakora
Prabhuji, Tum Moti, Hum Dhaga
Jaise Sonhe Milat Suhaga
Prabhuji, Tum Deepak Hum Baati,
Jaaki Jyoti Barai Dini Raati
Prabhuji, Tum Swami, Hum Dasa
Aisi Bhakti Karai Raidasa.'

The meaning of the poem. –

O Lord, if you are sandalwood, I am water.
The fragrance of that has infused in all parts of my body.
Lord, if you are a cloud, I am the peacock
Looking for you like a bird which looks at the moon.
Lord, if you are a pearl, I am the thread.
As the Borax mixes in the gold
Lord, if you are a lamp, I am the wick
The light is burning day and night
O Lord, if you are master, I am the servant
This is the devotion of Raidasa.

On the path of devotion, a devotee resorts to numerous means to reach the God, such as worship, meditation, penance, chanting the name of God, listening the stories of God, songs of God, the recitation of the verses of saints, purity of mind, contentment and desire to have glimpse of God. On the path of devotion, a devotee has keen desire to meet his master.

Saint Surdas ji says –

'Akhiyan hari darshan ki pyaasi,
Dekhyo chaahat kamal nayan ko,
Nisdin rehet udaasi.
Kesar tilak motin ki mala,
Vrindavan ke vaasi,
Neh lagaaye tyaag gaye trinsam,
Dal gye gal phaansi.
Kaahu ke man ki ko jaanat,
Logan ke man haasi,
Surdas prabhu tumhre daras bin,
Leho karwat kashi.
Akhiyan hari darshan ki pyaasi.'

This devotional song of saint Surdas coveys the longing for the glimpse of Lord Krishna.

Saint Surdas says: My eyes are thirsty for a glimpse of Krishna. I want to see the lotus-eyed Krishna but I don't see him which keeps me sad and restless every day.

Krishna, who uses saffron tilak and wears pearl necklace; Krishna who belongs to Vrindavan. After stealing my heart, he has left me like a worthless leaf of grass.

No one knows the pain which I suffer through on account of separation from Krishna.

People make fun of me, not knowing my pain. Krishna, without seeing you, I cannot rest. Saint Surdas further says that if I will not get your glimpse then it would be better for me to leave this body at Kashi.

Again, Surdas ji says –

'Mero Man Anat Kahan Sukh Pave.
Jaise udi Jahaj Kau Panchhi Puni Jahaj Pai vaye.
Kamalanain Ko Chhandi Mahatam aur Dev Ko Dhyave.
Paramagang Ko Chhodi Piyaso Durmati Koop Khonave.

Jin Madhukar Ambuj-ras Chakhyo, Kyon Karil-phal Khavo.
Surdas, Prabhu Kamadhenu Taji Chheri Kaun Duhave.'

Meaning of aforesaid couplet is that

Where else can my mind get joy?

A bird that lives on a ship might fly off but again lands back on the very ship.

Leaving the Glory of the Lotus-eyed Shri Krishna why should I run after any other God?

It would be foolishness to leave the purest water of Ganga and resort to a well to quench thirst.

When a bee has sucked the sweet nectar from a Lotus flower why would it taste the bitter guard?

Surdas Ji says 'Oh, my Lord! It would be foolishness to milk a goat in place of a wish-Cow with plenty of delicious milk.

Saint Meera Bai tells her Lord, Shri Krishna -

'Manmohan kanha vinati karoon din rain
Rah take mere nain
Ab to daras dedo kunj Bihari
Manva hai bechain
Sneh ki dori tum sang jori
Humse to nahi jaavegi todi
Hey murali dhar Krishna murari
Tanik Na aave chain
Raah take mere nain
Ab to daras dedo kunj Bihari.'

Meaning of above couplet of saint Meera-

'Oh, my Lord Krishna! I beg to you day and night and my eyes are waiting for you,

Now please give me your glimpse because my mind is restless for you.

Oh, my Krishna! I have tied the thread of love with you, it would be impossible for me to break it.

Oh, loveable Lord Krishna! I don't find peace without you.

My eyes are waiting for your arrival,

Now you, please don't delay, come soon and give me your glimpse.'

The aforesaid poems of Saint Surdas and Meera Bai show that they were in the state of complete devotion to God. The acute desire of the devotees to meet God is Bhakti Yoga. In this situation the mind of a devotee becomes completely detached from worldly desires and the mind and heart become pure like the water of Gangotri.

Saint Tulsi Das has said about the saints who have reached such state,

'Vishay alampat sheel gunakar, par dukh dukh sukh sukh dekhe par
Sam abhut ripu bimad biragi, lobhamarash harash bhay tyagi.'

That is, the saints who do not indulge in worldly things are mines of modesty and virtues. They get saddened by others sorrow and become happy from others happiness. They are always in the state of equanimity. They do not have enmity with anyone. They are always absorbed in quietness and keep away from ego, greed, anger and fear.

The period of fourteenth century to the sixteenth century is known as the Bhakti era in Indian history. This period is also called saint era. During this period, many great saints were born in different parts of India. They taught devotion to God through their teachings. They also spread the light of knowledge among the ignorant and lower society and told the people to come out of the caste captivity and untouchability. They said that those who remember God go near him. These saints advised the people that if they want to come out of their suffering then they must surrender before God. The saints told the people that your mind always deceives you and pulls you towards the worldly desires. Your mind distracts you from the right path. If you surrender your life before God, then he will surely drive you out of this illusionary world and you will get real happiness.

In Bhakti Yoga, the seeker begins to realize that the man is just like a puppet in the hands of the divine. Everything happens by God's will. With complete devotion to the God the sorrows of devotees are removed. The devotee also considers sorrow as the will of God due to which he gets infinite bliss.

Saint Tulsi Das says –

'Sakal kamna heen je Ram bhakti me leen,
Nam suprem Piyush driday tinhun kiye man meen.'

That is, those who are devoid of all kinds of desires and are engaged in the devotion of Rama, those who have kept their minds like fishes in the nectar like lake of lord Rama, such type of devotees do not want to be separated from it even for a single moment.

Saint Kabir says –

'Bhakti pran se hot hai, man de kijiye bhav,
Parmatam partit me yah tan jaye to jaye.'

It means that devotion is done with dedication and for that one should have the feeling in mind and heart. Even if one has to sacrifice his body for the devotion to God, let this body perishes.

Saint Narasimha Mehta (Narsi Mehta), born in Gujarat in the fifteenth century, used to say that a true Narayana (Lord Vishnu) devotee should have the following qualities. He is telling through this poem –

'Vaishnav Jan to tene kahiye je peed paraayi jaane re
Par-dukkhe upkaar kare toye man abhimaan Na aane re
SakaL lok maan sahune vande ninda Na kare keni re
Vaach kaachh man nishchaL raakhe dhan-dhan janani teni re
Sam-drishti ne trishna tyaagi par-stree jene maat re

Jivha thaki asatya Na bole par-dhan nav jhaalee haath re
Moh-maya vyaape nahi jene drirh vairaagya Jena man maa re
Ram naam shoon taali laagi sakaL tirath tena tan maa re
Van-lobhi ne kapat-rahit chhe kaam-krodh nivaarya re
Bhane Narsaiyyo tenun darshan karta kul ekoter taarya re.'

The meaning of aforesaid devotional poem is that

One is the real Vaishnav (Devotee of Lord Vishnu) who knows the pain of others.

He does good to others without letting pride enter in his mind.

A Vaishnav, tolerates and praises the entire world.

Does not speak bad words to others, Keeps his promises, actions and thoughts pure,

The mother of such Vaishnava is blessed indeed.

A Vaishnav sees everybody equally, rejects greed and avarice,

Respects women as he respects his own mother,

His tongue may get tired if he will utter untruth,

He never touches the property of others.

A true Vaishnav does not succumb to worldly attachments,

He has renounced all kinds of lust and anger.

The poet Narsi would like to see such a person by whose glimpse,

The entire family gets salvation.

There were differences among these saints regarding the nature of God. Some saints believed in Saguna Bhakti i.e., the God in form. The prominent saints like Ramanand and Goswami Tulsi Das were the devotees of Lord Rama whereas saints like Surdas, Mirabai, Jayadeva, Narsi Mehta, Narottam Das and Chaitanya Mahaprabhu were the devotees of Lord Krishna. In South India, while Alvars saints were devotees of Lord Vishnu (Narayana), the Nayanar saints were devotees of Lord Shiva.

Nirguna Bhakti i.e., faith in the formless God - Saint Kabir Das, Saint Kabir Das's son Saint Kamal Das, Saint Ravidas, Saint

Dharmadas, Guru Nanak, Saint Maluka Das and Saint Haridas were devotees of formless God.

Saint Kabir used to chant the name of Rama but saint Kabir's Rama was not son of King Dasharatha but the God who is all pervasive and omnipresent.

Saint Kabir says –

'Ek Ram Dashrath ka Beta, Ek Ram jo ghat ghat betha.
Ek Ram ka sakal Pasara, Ek Ram Jo sab se nyara.'

That is, there was one Rama who was the son of Raghuvanshi Kshatriya king Dasharatha. A Rama who is a consciousness in every living being, a Rama who is the eternal indestructible Brahman and the entire universe is within him and one Rama is the most unique i.e., eternal, infinite truth and its original form is cosmic consciousness.

Due to polytheism in Hinduism, there is confusion among many sadhakas. It leads to lack of concentrate in one God and due to this there is dearth of bhakti yoga. In Bhakti Yoga, the worshipers of the Saguna form should meditate in one idol or form, this leads to concentration, determination and full devotion. With this, the sadhaka can enjoy the fruits of devotion. For this reason, while Saint Tulsi Das was a devotee of Shri Rama, Saint Surdas, Saint Meera Bai and Chaitanya Mahaprabhu were the devotees of Shri Krishna. While Maharishi Sandipani, Maharishi Markandeya and Gorakhnath, (a saint of the Nath sect) were the devotees of Lord Shiva and Sri Ramakrishna Paramahamsa was devotee of Goddess Kali.

According to some saints there is no difference between Saguna devotion (form worship) and Nirguna devotion (formless worship). The aim of both ways is to realise God.

Saint Tulsi Das says -

'Sagunhi nirgunhi nahi kuchh bheda gawahi muni puran, buddh bheda,
Agun Arup Alakh Aj Joi, Bhagat Prem Vash Sagun Hoi.'

That is, there is no difference between Saguna and Nirguna, as it has been said by Muni, Gyani, Vedas and Puranas, that which is Nirguna, formless, invisible and unborn becomes ostensible under the love of devotees.

Saint Surdas is telling in his 'Sur Sagar' that Nirguna Bhakti is a difficult path which is not easy for everyone. –

'Avigat Gati Kachhu Kahati N Aavai;
Jyo Goongo Meethe Phal Kee Ras Antargat Hee Bhaavai
Param Svaadu Sabahee Ju Nirantar Amit Tosh Upajaavai;
Man vanee Ko Agam Agochar So Jaane Jo Paavai
Roop Raikh Gun Jaati Jugati Binu Niraalanb Man Chakrit Dhaavai;
Sab Bidhi Agam Bichaarahi Taato Soor Sagun Leelaa Pad Gaavai.'

Poet Surdas says that it is very difficult to describe the formless God because nothing can be said about this situation.

Giving further example, Surdas says that after eating delicious fruits, the dumb person cannot say about the taste of the fruits. He just enjoys the fruit. In the same way, the devotee gets the pleasure of the formless God internally. He is unable to describe it to anyone.

The worshiper of the formless Brahma enjoys a lot of pleasure and immense satisfaction. But it is not easy for everyone to know this because it cannot be known by the senses.

The formless Brahma has neither any form nor shape. Nor he has any definite characteristics. Nor is there any caste. Nor can he be achieved by any device. In such a situation, where will the worshiper keep wandering without any basis? The formless Brahma is inaccessible for the ordinary man.

In such a situation, Surdas says that after having thought over these entire situations he decided to sing devotional song of Saguna Leela of lord shri Krishna.

However, the great saint Kabir used to emphasize on formless devotion and used to say that God has no colour, no form, no caste, no shape, neither he takes birth nor he can die, he is Immortal, imperceptible, formless and eternal.

Saint Kabir says while emphasizing on the worship of Nirguna Rama.

'Nirgun Ram Japahu re Bhai,
Avigat Ram gati laki na jahi.'

"O brother chant the name of nirgun Rama.
The action of invisible Rama cannot be seen."

The Upanishads also put stress on the formless God. In the 'Mundaka Upanishad' it is said –

"yattadadreśyamagrāhyamagotramavarṇa-
macakṣuḥśrotraṃ tadapāṇipādam.
nityaṃ vibhuṃ sarvagataṃ susūkṣmaṃ
tadavyayaṃ yadbhūtayoniṃ paripaśyanti dhīrāḥ."

That which is invisible (being beyond the sensory organs and mind) and which can never be grasped by the mind and sensual organs, which cannot be seized, which has no origin, which has no properties, which has neither ear nor eye, which has neither hands nor feet, which is eternal, diversely manifested, all-pervading, extremely subtle and the source of all creation. The wise men see this Brahman everywhere and in every being. (Mundaka Upanishad - Verse 1.1.6)

In the Bhagavad Gita, Shri Krishna is telling Arjuna about bhakti yoga –

'Anapekṣhaḥ śhuchir dakṣha udāsīno gata-vyathaḥ
Sarvārambha-parityāgī yo mad-bhaktaḥ sa me priyaḥ.'

He who has no desires, who is pure, who is dextrous, who is impartial, who is free from fear, who has renounced every undertaking-such a devotee of mine is dear to me. (Bhagavad Gita - 12/16)

Thus, the basis of devotion is complete surrender to God. In devotion to God, the mind, intellect and body have to be concentrated on God then the Prasad of God i.e., the fruit of the devotion can be received. Once the person has taken the ecstasy of devotion, he will despise worldly and sensual pleasure.

13
KARMA YOGA

Karma is very important in human life. Therefore, it is necessary for every human being to understand the nuances of 'karma'. Karma is the basis of human life cycle. The future of an individual will depend on the karma of present life. Good deeds done by a person determine the good direction of life. Karma produces the capital of present life and the next life. Every human being has to bear the fruits of karma in this life or in the future in terms of destiny, just as the bank balance sheet or the summery of statement of deposits and withdrawals of money. Similarly, the work done by a person prepares the balance sheet of his life. It is said that even God does not interfere in the matter of karma. Even Shri Rama and Shri Krishna had to bear the fruits of their karma. Shri Rama also had to face many sufferings in exile and Shri Krishna had to be killed by the arrow of the hunter. It is said that when Shri Krishna was in meditation while sitting in the forest, then a hunter named Ziru came. He saw the foot pad of Shri Krishna and thought that a deer was resting there. Thinking of hunting of the deer, the hunter shot an arrow and the arrow pierced the sole of Shri Krishna's feet. Hunter apologized to Shri Krishna with folded hands, but Shri Krishna said that it was not his fault. After uttering this, Shri Krishna gave up his life. The Saints have said that every human being has to bear the fruits of his karma. In the same way Devas also suffer the fruits of their karma. In the Treta Yuga, Rama hiding behind a tree killed Bali, brother of Sugriva with his arrows. In order to rectify that,

God made Bali a hunter and chose the similar death for Krishna who was incarnation of Rama.

While explaining the cycle of Karma saint Kabir says -

'Karam gaati tare nahi tari,
Guru Vashishta se pandit gyani, shodh ke lagan dhari
Sita haran maran Dasharatha ke bana me bipati pari,
Pandav jinke Krishna sarathi tin par vipati Pari,
Karam gati tare nahi tari.'

Saint Kabir says that the result of karma is irrevocable. It can never be stopped. He says that a knowledgeable guru like Vashishta had prepared the horoscope of Shri Rama after much research and he had also decided the auspicious time for the marriage of Rama with Sita, yet Rama had to face exile and his wife Sita was also kidnapped. Ram had to suffer many problems in the forest. In the meantime, Rama also had to suffer due to the death of King Dasharatha. Further, Saint Kabir says that Pandava's charioteer was Shri Krishna himself, yet Pandavas had to suffer a lot. In this way, everyone has to bear the fruits of 'karma' whether it is shri Rama, shri Krishna or Pandava. The result of karma is unalterable. It can never be stopped.

The rotating cycle of karma sometimes makes a person best and sometimes weak. At the time of the battle of Mahabharata, Arjuna was considered the greatest archer. Other warriors used to get frightened by the sound of Gandiva of Arjuna. The same Arjuna could not protect the gopis (young girls of yadavas) from the Bhils, (a kind of tribe). Goswami Tulsidas has described this incident.

'Tulsi nar ka kya bada, samay hot balwan
Bhila luta gopiya wahi Arjun wahi van.'

The 24th Tirthankara, Lord Vardhman Mahavira used to say that every action performed by the mind, words and the senses becomes engraved in the mind and the fruits of actions done by the senses have to be reaped. If there is maliciousness in one's mind and even if it is not implemented, it is still a karma done by the mind and it is sure to bear the consequences. Even in criminal law intention plays a crucial role. Lord Mahavira used to say that violence towards any creature can spoil the result of the karma, therefore, non-violence should be observed by mind, word and action.

Types of Karma: -

There are three types of Karma (actions) -

1. Sakam Karma (Attached Karma or karma for own benefit) - The karma which is done for livelihood or for ambition or for charity or for the attainment of joy or fame is called Sakam Karma. In these deeds, the selfishness of the person is involved. The self-gained karma binds the person due to the attachment to the result of karma. Though the results of good deeds are definitely good, but the deeds done with the desire of the results of the karma cannot liberate a person from the life cycle of rebirth, that is, through such actions one cannot attain salvation. To consider death as salvation is a big mistake. Death is just the end of this body. After the end of the body, the soul again takes another body, but after salvation there is end-of-life cycle. The path to attain moksha or kaivalya is not easy, but it is possible to attain moksha only after purifying the mind by eliminating all flaws deposited in subconscious and unconscious mind, through the continuous practice of meditation and following moral code of conducts.
2. Vikarma (forbidden karma) - Karma which is against the society and moral values, which is also called sinful karma. Such sinful actions lead man to downfall and such a person is born in the next life to a lower realm as animal or insect.
3. Akram (nishkam or detached karma) - Akram means detached karma, that is, karma which is completely devoid of the desire for the fruit of the karma. Totally unattached karma is nishkam karma and such karma can be called karma yoga. In

> Karmayoga, a person performs actions without attachment to the results of Karma, that is, he remains detached to the consequences arising out of Karma. The work done with virtuous spirit without any longing for profit or loss, victory-defeat, fame-condemnation, etc.is called 'Karma Yoga' and a person who performs such detached action is called 'Karmayogi.'

There have been many karmayogis in history such as Satyavadi King Harishchandra, Mithila King Janaka, king Shivi of Ushi Nagar and King Vikramaditya of Ujjain.

Although in Bhagavad Gita, there has been a detailed discussion on Janana, devotion and Karma Yoga. However, special emphasis has been given on the 'Karma Yoga.' The story in the background of the Bhagavad Gita is that despite making all efforts, Duryodhana flatly refused to give even five villages to the Pandavas. The arrogant Duryodhana clearly told Shri Krishna that he would not give land even equal to the tip of a needle to the Pandavas and what to talk of five villages? After the attempt to denude Draupadi by Dushasana in a large gathering, several abuses and torture to the Pandavas, categorical refusal to give five villages and the rejection of all attempts of compromise, the Pandavas were left with no other option but to fight against Kauravas. However, Arjuna was not ready for the battle. Arjuna was depressed but Shri Krishna wanted to remove Arjuna's sadness, attachment and ignorance. Lord Shri Krishna brought awareness in the mind of Arjuna about the injustice and unrighteousness and convinced him to fight the battle against unrighteousness and injustice. Shri Krishna thought that if injustice and unrighteousness is not redressed, then malpractices and atrocities will increase in the society and country and there will be increase of demonic tendencies on this earth which will encourage unrighteousness and sin.

The entire Bhagavad Gita has eighteen chapters and seven hundred (700) verses, which are in Sanskrit language. In this, jnana, devotion and spiritual topics have been discussed in detail, but the central point of the Bhagavad Gita is - to bring Arjuna out of dejection and to make him realize his duty.

Lord Shri Krishna tried to bring Arjuna out of ignorance and delusion through many examples and reasoned dialogue and said that without action this life cannot be imagined. A human cannot live even for a single moment without karma. In this world, every human being is doing his work at every moment through his senses. All living beings act according to their nature and qualities and lead their lives. 'Oh, Arjuna! You are a Kshatriya (soldier), so it is your paramount duty to protect the country and society. If you run away from your duty, you will be a part of failure all your life and future generation will ridicule you by calling you a coward.'

Shri Krishna further said that fighting the war against the Kauravas is not your personal battle, but it is a crusade. Shri Krishna explains to Arjun and says that oh, Parth! Just think over that those who were intoxicated of power, could not protect the honour of Draupadi, the queen of Indraprastha, then how would they protect the honour and respect of a common woman? Lord Krishna encouraged Arjuna and advised him to fight this battle like a karma yogi without any fear, attachment and hatred because affection arising out of attachment and aversion binds the person in bondage of action which is a hindrance to salvation. Therefore, fight the war devoid of attachment, affection and hatred. Oh Arjuna! Perform your duties while being established in yoga, renouncing attachment and have even -temperament in success and failure. The evenness of mind is called yoga. (Bhagavad Gita - 2/48)

Lord Shri Krishna further explains to Arjuna that the fear of death is also an illusion, because only the body dies, the soul (consciousness) is immortal and eternal, it is a part of God and it is imperishable. The soul renounces one body and takes another body just as a man discards old clothes and puts on new clothes. (Bhagavat Gita -2/22), Therefore you forget the fear of death and fight.

Lord Shri Krishna further says that oh, Arjuna! All the immovable and movable in this world are in fact impermanent by being perishable and transitory, (B.G.-13/26) therefore, leave your worries and do your duty by becoming united with God.

Oh Arjuna! Whenever there is decline of righteousness and increase of unrighteousness, I create my form i.e., manifest myself to save sages and destroy those who do evil deeds in order to establish dharma. To do this, I appear in every age. (Bhagavad Gita - 4/ 6, 8). Oh Arjuna! Hypocrisy, arrogance, conceit, anger, rigidity and ignorance all are symptoms of demonic tendencies. (Bhagvat Gita – (16/4). Therefore, you fight against these Kauravas of demonic nature, so that this earth can be free from sin. Keeping in mind the public interest, one who acts with full devotion to God without attachment or malice to anyone does not get trapped in the bondage of karma and he attains salvation by acquiring knowledge. This is why, you should always do your duty without attachment because doing work without attachment one attains God (Bhagavad Gita-3/19).

In fact, Karmayoga is not an easy path, but a difficult path. Here a person has a pure mind free from any attachment, hatred or desire. In a nutshell desireless karma is 'karma yoga.'

14
RAJA YOGA

'Raja Yoga' is called the king of all yoga systems, because some elements of all yoga systems are definitely found in it. The author of Raja Yoga is considered to be Maharishi Patanjali, who compiled yoga science in 195 sutras around the second century AD. He gave yoga a new dimension. It is also known as 'Patanjali Yoga Sutra.'

The aim of Raja Yoga is the inhibition (nirodhaḥ) of the modifications (vṛtti) of the mind. There are five forms of ground or base (Cittabhumi), or the state of mind, which are as follows -

1. Kshipta, (Restless or distracted state of mind or the state of Monkey mind)
2. Mudda (a state of laziness, dull or infatuated state, the state of Donkey mind)
3. Vikshipta (state of irregular steady or temporary concentration, Butterfly Mind).
4. Ekagra (One pointed state or concentration state, candle mind, focused mind, On one point), and
5. Nirudha – (Restrained state, fully concentrated mind.
    1. In the state of kshipta, the mind works like monkey mind. Totally restless jumping from one subject to another, unable to stay on one point, wavering or distracted mind.
    2. In the state of mudda, the mind becomes sleepy, dull, and lethargic. It does not want to perform duty. Mind wants to

engage in unwanted things and remain in ignorance or in desperation.

3. Vikshipta or occasionally steady mind, the temporary stability of mind, influenced by confusion. Mind works like butterfly which stays for some time on one flower and then moves to another flower.
4. Ekagra or one-pointed. The one-pointed mind influenced by pure Sattva is able to withdraw from all objects i.e., totally introverted, to remain focussed on one object. It is the first step of yoga which is called 'Samprajnata samadhi', 'Samprajnata' means Samadhi with 'Prajna' or highest wisdom.
5. Niruddha or restrained. The restrained mind also influenced by pure Sattva, stop all mental modifications i.e., there is complete suspension of all mental modes and sub-conscious dispositions. It is fully concentrated state of mind. It is also called wakeup state or state of 'Asamprajnata samadhi.'

For example, when a practitioner of meditation closes his eyes and concentrates on the breathing. After some time, the mind starts to calm down and the breathing starts slowing down. A state of deep meditation comes when the practitioner does not know about breath. The mind becomes still. This stage is called the state of 'emptiness.' In this state, the sadhaka experiences peace and bliss.

Human mind is fickle by nature. Although every man is considered a repository of advanced knowledge and power, but the capriciousness of the mind destroys his mental and physical energy. Raja Yoga tries to awaken the human being through the concentration of the mind. It tries to combine the scattered powers of the seeker to achieve desired goal. With continuous practice of 'Raja Yoga', the five tribulations namely, ignorance, ego, attachment, malice and fear are gradually eliminated. These five tribulations make human life miserable.

The Raja Yoga of Maharishi Patanjali is also known as 'Ashtanga

Yoga.' There are eight parts (limbs) of this yoga, i.e., Yama (self-control), Niyama (discipline), asana (exercise of various bodily organs), pranayama (breathing exercises, such as, anulom-vilom (inhaling from one nostril and exhaling from the other) Kapalabhati or Bhastrika), Pratyahara (withdrawal of mind and senses from outside i.e., detachment from external things), Dharana (one point concentration), meditation and samadhi.

'Yama' means moral code of conduct like nonviolence, truthfulness, non-stealing, chastity, non-possessiveness of excessive wealth than minimum requirement, forgiveness, patience, compassion, non-hypocrisy and measured diet. 'Niyama' is the internal code for a sadhaka i.e., purity of mind and body, contentment, tapa (self-control), self-study (self-inspection), generosity, humility, conciliatory approach in conflicting ideas, pursuit for spiritual knowledge and reverence for God. 'Asana' is the exercise of physical organs so that the body remains fit and healthy. 'Pranayama' is breathing exercise, 'Pratyahara' means detachment of mind and senses from outside. Then concentration of mind on one point, meditation and finally samadhi. In this, the first five subjects i.e., Yama, Niyama, Asana, Pranayama and Pratyahara are 'external means, while Dharana (concentration), meditation and samadhi are 'internal means.' The ultimate goal of Maharishi Patanjali's Ashtanga Yoga is to achieve Kaivalya. 'Kaivalya' is derived from the word 'Kevala' of Sanskrit language, which means alone, that is, the state of connection of mind only with the soul. The purpose of Ashtanga yoga is to attain the state of samadhi by meditation and to remove sexual desire, anger, greed, ego, attachment and hatred from the mind.

The state of 'Kaivalya' is an extraordinary state and one has to practice meditation continuously to achieve it. After attaining the state of Kaivalya, man gets rid of the cycle of life and death forever. The person gets rid of the bondage of karma. The mind chaos is the cause of suffering. The aim of ashtanga yoga is to eliminate mental modifications and sufferings.

15
VIPASSANA MEDITATION

Day by day increasing crime, violence, murder, rape, theft, falsehood, deceit, domestic discord, social unrest, moral turpitude, mental distress and depression have made the human life miserable. However, human beings are solely responsible for all these evils. The Ignorance is the main cause of these malaises.

The religious scriptures and the religious teachers are of the view that sexual desires, anger, greed, ego, attachment and hatred are the causes of human suffering, but these scriptures and religious teachers have no remedy for these evils created by human beings. It is known fact that the mind is polluted by anger. There is a kind of chemical secretion inside the mind that makes the person sad, but people do not know how to stop the anger. This is the reason that the man has been committing misdeed by anger, greed or other forms of violence since centuries. These misdeeds done by human beings have destroyed the peace and happiness of all. But how to end such tendencies is a big challenge before human beings.

Lord Buddha used to say that we are made by our thoughts. Everything happens as we think. When we are of pure mind, then the joy follows us like shadow as the wheels of bullock carts follow the strings of the oxen.

Our mind is the originator of bad and good thoughts. This is why Saint Kabir says,

'Mann ke mate na chaliye, Mann ke mate anek
Jo Mann par aswar hai, so sadhu koi ek.'

Don't go as per the view of mind, there are many views of mind
One who has control over the mind is a saint of rare quality.

In the Bhagavad Gita, while giving lecture on yoga to Arjuna, Shri Krishna said that it is necessary to subdue the mind for yoga. Then Arjun says to Shri Krishna-

'Chañchalaṁ hi manaḥ kṛiṣhṇa pramāthi balavad dṛiḍham
Tasyāhaṁ nigrahaṁ manye vāyoriva su-duṣhkaram.'

"Hey Shri Krishna! This mind is very fickle, firm and strong. Therefore, to control it is a very difficult task like stopping the air." (Bhagavad Gita - 6/34)

To understand the mind, it is necessary to understand the science of the mind. According to psychology, by repeatedly listening, seeing or thinking about any object or subject, the habit of the mind becomes the same. That is, conditioning of mind takes place. In other words, it can be said that the mind's habit of thinking or pattern goes in the same direction, for example, a person who is an alcoholic or a smoker repeatedly gets addicted to alcohol or smoking by practice. On seeing alcohol or cigarettes, alcoholic or cigarette smokers get attracted to it. Russian Nobel Prize winner Ivan Pavlov's theory of conditioning is quite famous. He has said that doing any task continuously makes the mind of a man or animal habitual, such as an untrained horse initially does not let the master to sit on its back and creates lots of troubles for the cavalryman. But the horseman gets victory over the horse after constant training. After giving continuous training, the cavalryman makes the horse of his own and the horse becomes loyal to the horseman and starts following the gestures of its master. Human mind also works similarly. Lord Buddha used to say that we become what we think.

In the Bhagavad Gita, Shri Krishna is explaining this –

'Dhyāyato viṣhayān puṁsaḥ saṅgas teṣhūpajāyate
Saṅgāt sañjāyate kāmaḥ kāmāt krodho 'bhijāyate.'

While contemplating on the objects of the senses, one develops attachment to them. Attachment leads to desire, and from desire arises anger. (Bhagavad Gita - 2/62)

Wencher, (veshyagami), drunkards or addicts become habitual due to repeated thinking about those objects. Such people can also do all kinds of misdeeds to fulfil their habits, because they have become slave of their mind.

Saint Kabir says –

'Yeh Mann maila neech hai, neech karam suhai
Amrit chharai Mann karai, vishai priti so khaye.'

This mind is dirty and lowly, likes low things
Knowingly leaves the nectar and goes after sensual pleasures.

Finally, these bad habits or instincts lead to suffering. Then how can a man get rid of his bad habit or instincts? Although there are many ways like devotional yoga, karmayoga and other means but these are not permanent solution or means to subdue the mind. Due to the above means, the mind remains calm for a while, but when the senses come in contact with any object, again it gets attracted and the control is lost. It is not easy to break the magic-net of the mind.

According to renowned psychologist Sigmund Freud, the human mind is composed of three layers, namely, conscious, subconscious and unconscious mind. The unfulfilled desires and events of life are dumped in the subconscious and unconscious mind and they float like iceberg in our mind. They also come in our dreams and occasionally create tribulation in the mind.

There are many examples in mythological stories when a sage cursed someone in anger. The story of sage Durvasha is prevalent. Again, the austerities of sages were ruined by Indra's fairies like Rambha, Maneka. The story of sage Vishwamitra is quite popular. These so-called sages or mahatmas did not conquer their anger or lust. A person cannot be called mahatma or saint if he has not conquered the mind and senses.

There are many examples of such great men in history who have completely destroyed all their tribulations, vices or lusts like sexual desires, anger, greed, ego, attachment and hatred and became 'arhat' or 'arihanta'. Lord Vardhman Mahavira is called Jitendriya, Arihanta or Kevali. Lord Buddha is called Tathagata, Arhat or Param Bodhi.

Lord Buddha got the ultimate knowledge, enlightenment, by subduing his senses and mind. He understood the nature of the mind like a psychiatrist and said that the root cause of human suffering is ignorance created by the mind. Buddha used to say that, the mind is the instigator of all the bad tendencies. It is the individual's own mind, not his enemy, who encourages him for evil deeds. Therefore, one should control the mind through regular practice of vipassana.

Lord Buddha further said that it is better to conquer our own mind than to win thousand battles. Then the victory will be ours. It cannot be taken away by anyone. Lord Buddha suggested Vipassana Meditation to get rid of the vices of the mind and to destroy the flaws deposited inside the sub conscious mind. He said that continuous exercise of Vipassana will purify the mind. Once the mind is purified, then the feeling of 'brahma vihara' like peace, joy and compassion would crop up in the mind.

The Vipassana meditation method is described in the 'Saptipathana Sutta' of Majjhimnikaya of the Buddhist text. Vipassana meditation was started by Lord Buddha. It is purely a science of mind. Before starting Vipassana, every practitioner is required to observe Panchsheela,i.e, five code of conduct namely, 1 - Do not commit violence, 2 - Do not steal, 3 – Maintain celibacy, 4- Do not lie and 5 - Do not take any kind of intoxication.

The word 'Vipassana' is derived from Pali language which means to watch through your inner vision, to observe the thoughts going in the mind and to see the sensations going on in the body as a witness. It is to watch the movement of the breath, and the heartbeat, inside the body. In vipassana one has to just observe minutely and continuously the movements inside the body and mind with closed eyes.

Types of Vipassana -

There are many types of Vipassana. It is said that Lord Buddha told his monks about 52 types of Vipassana meditation method. Some of the major Vipassana meditations are as follows -

1. Anapan Sati Meditation - This is the first stage of Vipassana meditation. In this, the practitioner has to observe the movement of breath. Keeping the mind focused and watching the movement of breath through both the nostrils carefully is called anapanasati meditation.
2. Kayanupassana -Watching one's own body from top to bottom in meditation. Seeing the whole body from insight vision is called Kayanupassana.
3. Vedanupassana - Through this meditation method one has to see the sensations of the body. If there is itching on the skin, it is not to be rubbed, but just feel the itching. After a while, that itching will cease on its own. Change is the eternal law of nature. Everything is temporary.
4. Chittanupassana - In this meditation, one has to observe the thoughts of the mind, one has to observe how many thoughts keep coming and going in the mind. Cittanupassana is to watch those thoughts by being neutral.
5. Dhammanupassana - Observing the natural activities inside our body like how the supply of breath is going into the micro tubes of each organ. To feel the sky element of the body, i.e., to get experience of emptiness in the state of deep meditation where one feel that 'I am not a body' but the 'consciousness.'
6. Chakra Meditation - This meditation is practiced in some Buddhist sects. Through this meditation, the practitioners meditate on their seven chakras (Kundalini) one by one. Seven Chakras i.e., 1- Root chakra, (Muladhara Chakra, near the anus of the body), 2- Sacral chakra (Swadhisthana Chakra, near the penis), 3- Solar plexus chakra, (Manipur Chakra, near the navel), 4- Heart chakra, (Anhad Chakra near the heart), 5- Throat chakra, (Vishudha Chakra, Near the throat),6- Third

eye chakra, (Aagya chakra located near bhrakuti), 7- Crown chakra, (sahastrar chakra located in the lower part of the head).

It is said that the 'life energy' lies at the base of the spine (root chakra), coiled like a snake. In Kundalini meditation, one can awake this energy and achieve enlightenment through a combination of techniques, including: deep breathing.

It is further said that the person who has awakened the Sahastrar Chakra attains eight Siddhies (Ashtasiddhi) i.e., Anima, Mahima, Laghima, Garima, Prapti, Prakamya, Ishitva and Vashitva. However, the method of Kundalini awakening has not been mentioned in Buddhist literature. Many Buddhist sects, especially Buddhist monks of Tibet, perform many miraculous actions such as lifting their bodies in the air by these siddhis. It is said that Lord Buddha knew many miracles. The description of his miracle is found in many Buddhist texts. But Lord Buddha was strongly against the performance of these miracles. He used to say that due to these miracles, the real religion will collapse and people will start believing the miracle as religion and they will be again trapped in the delusion.

Once Buddha was asked by someone, "Oh, Shakya Muni! what have you received by doing Vipassana meditation for so many years? "He replied that, "through these meditation methods 'I have found peace of mind, purity, bliss and wisdom (jnana) and I have attained freedom from anger, craving, attachment, ego and various kinds of vices. Now I feel a sense of complete freedom."

THIRD CHAPTER - SPIRITUALITY

16
SPIRITUALITY

Almost all religions have two elements, that is, external and internal element. The external elements of religion are the rituals and customs of that religion, whereas the internal element of religion is the basic essence of religion. We may say that the basic essence is the actual religion. As in the coconut, kernel is its essence and the fibrous shell of coconut is just outer layer or cover of the fruit. The internal element of religion is the spiritual element. The spiritual elements of religion are found in the sacred texts of the religions such as the essence of Hinduism can be found in Bhagavad Gita and Upanishads. Similarly, essence of Buddhism is found in Sutta Pitaka and Abhidhamma Pitaka. But often people do not pay attention to the metaphysics and usually follow rituals, festivals, customs and other traditions as religion. Therefore, due to prevalence of the external elements of religion, the basic element of religion i.e., its spiritual element has gone in oblivion and have become obscure. Goswami Tulsidas has put the same thing beautifully in the following lines -

'Harit bhoomi trin sankul samujhi parahi nahi panth,
Jimi pakhand vad te gupt hoi sadagranth.'

It means, just as the track passing through the agricultural land is not visible due to the excessive growth of grass during the rainy season, in the same way, due to the propagation of rituals or hypocrisy, the holy texts have become obscured.

Spirituality is to know about oneself, about own soul or consciousness. In other words, spirituality is to know about oneself and the subtle metaphysical mysteries. The irony of this world is that human beings know many things of the world but remain ignorant about self. Whether a Hindu, a Muslim, a Christian, a Sikh, a Buddhist or a Jain, all human beings are made by the same elements. Everyone's body is made of seven dhatu namely,

Rasa Dhatu: Plasma/lymph fluid,
Rakta Dhatu: Blood,
Mansa Dhatu: Muscles,
Meda Dhatu: Fat,
Asthi Dhatu: Bones,
Majja Dhatu: Bone marrow,
Shukra Dhatu: Reproductive fluid or Semen.

The body of all human beings is made of five elements i.e., soil (bones and flesh), water, fire, air and emptiness inside the body, which is called 'Akash element'. Actually, all the elements of the human body are made of microscopic molecules. There are invisible spaces between the joints of these molecules. This space is called emptiness. The consciousness of every human being is composed of the Panch Vayus (5 winds) i.e., Prana, Apana, Udaan, smana and vyana. 'Va' means 'motion' or 'that which flows' (Prana and Pranayama). The vayus represent the flow of subtle energy within the 5 Koshas. This gives energy to the body without which there would be no life.

Spirituality enables a person to come out of the ignorance and get awaken. But spirituality can only be followed by pursuing meditation, Vipassana and contemplation. The knowledge of the seven chakras inside the body i.e., Muladhara, Swadhisthan, Manipur, Anhad, vishudha, Aagya and Sahastrar Chakras and five Koshas i.e., Annamaya, Pranamaya, Manomaya, Vigyanamaya and Anandamaya Koshas are the further steps to understand oneself.

Regardless of the religion every man has the same life cycle, that is, the course of birth and death is the same. This mortal body made of five elements, will assimilate into five elements of nature, when the consciousness (soul) will leave this body. This is an unalterable rule of nature. Nature has not made distinction between human beings namely, caste or communal differences but these differences are man-made due to selfishness, arrogance and ignorance. Many religions or sects have pushed human beings into the darkness of ignorance. Some books of some religions have said absurd and unscientific things, due to which all kinds of misconceptions have arisen. Since the wisdom is not awakened in majority of the people, they do not understand the cosmic or natural realities. Furthermore, they start hating each other by falling into the narrow disputes created by communal, ethnic, linguistic or nationalistic differences. But a spiritually awakened person treats everyone equally regardless of caste, creed, region or religion, because every creature is the creation of the same God or nature, and all living beings have the same consciousness.

Actually, spirituality teaches us to understand oneself by becoming introvert, but the people watch or sense external things through five senses. But spirituality is not external, it is to be aware of the inner self. One can understand the consciousness through meditation or by becoming introvert. Right knowledge is possible only through meditation or contemplation.

Broadly, there are two types of knowledge i.e. Apara Gyan and Para Gyan (knowledge derived from senses & extra sensory knowledge). The subjects, which are known by the senses, are called apara Gyan, (lower knowledge) but the knowledge which is received by extra senses or by telepathy or through deep meditation is called para jnana which is higher knowledge. There are five types of knowledge, namely mati Gyan which is received by the senses, shruti Gyan which is acquired by listening, Avadhi jnana is divine knowledge attained by higher meditation, Manparyaya (extra sensory knowledge), i.e., knowledge of knowing the mind of another person and Kaivalya jnana which is the realization of ultimate truth. Kaivalya Gyan is the supreme knowledge through which a person can know about abstract, consciousness,

Maya, Brahma, Moksha, past lives and the eternal rules of the universe. After attainment of Kaivalya jnana, nothing is left to be known in this world. Maharishi Patanjali has discussed Kaivalya Gyan in the fourth chapter of his Yoga Sutra. This Kaivalya knowledge was received by Lord Buddha and Lord Mahavira after deep meditation.

One question is often asked, that why in this world some people have worst nature than animals? Every human being look alike by appearance but some human beings have beastly character.

Hindi Poet Dinkar beautifully put this,

'Jhad gaye punchh romant jhade, pashuta ka jhadna baki hai, tan bahar bahar sawar chuka man ka sawarana baki hai.' In fact, the human beings have gradually evolved from monkey. They have ceded the hair of monkey but the inside is still animal like. The human beings have decorated themselves with beautiful clothes but the mind is still to be purified. In the Bhagavad Gita, Lord Krishna says that hypocrisy, arrogance, pride, anger, harsh speech and ignorance are all signs of devilish instinct, (Bhagavad Gita-16 / 4-5). Why does man have devilish instincts? Maharishi Kapil had answered this. This has also been reiterated by Bhagavad Gita. According to Samkhya doctrine, man is of three kinds of nature i.e., tamoguni, rajoguni and satoguni. The person of tamo guna remains in an unconscious state of mind and his mind is covered with shortcomings. His behaviour is beastly. Such people are thieves, burglars, rapists, drug addicts and have other immoral qualities. Such people only run after the sensual pleasures.

Razo guni are those who run after power and wealth, like businessmen, industrialists, politicians or persons in power. Such people are full of ego and have obsession for luxury. They do every work in the world for their material progress and selfish motive, even charitable works are done with selfish motives to get fame and to cover their misdeeds. Such people come to this world again and again due to selfishness and attachment. Sato guni are those who understand the true nature of this world. This world is in fact a mortuary (mrityulok) and everything in this world is temporary but due to Maya (Illusion) human beings are attached to this samsara. Satoguni live like hermit by detaching their mind and senses from external things.

Most of the people in this world live in unconscious state and do not understand the truth of this world that this world is a temporary shelter. As long as one live in this world, one should live with peace and joy, keep one's conduct pure, so that one does not have to regret in the last moment of life for the bad karma. In the absence of right knowledge, man indulges in bad deeds. The social and religious practices of the world also keep human beings in darkness. To get out of these social, cultural and communal darkness, one should search the truth through right knowledge, i.e., through independent inquiry and contemplation.

Plato, the great philosopher of Greece, has tried to explain through his book 'Allegory of Cave' (Cave Metaphor) that how people live in ignorance and die in ignorance. In this metaphorical story, some prisoners have been imagined. Since their childhood these prisoners have been tied in a dark cave with stone straps, due to this, they cannot move their heads and cannot even see the sidewalls. They can only see the front wall of the cave. There is fire burning behind the prisoners and some puppets are dancing in front of the fire, whose shadows are seen on the front wall of the cave. The shadows of the puppets and the echo of outer sound of the cave, appear as genuine to the prisoners of the cave. Those prisoners have accepted it as the truth.

It is further narrated in the story that once a prisoner got freed from the cave, and he came out of that dark cave and saw the sunlight and the scenery of nature in the open sky, in broad daylight. He was very surprised and now he realised that what he had seen till now was just an illusion, the truth is something else. But if that prisoner would narrate about his outside experience to those prisoners who were still inside the cave, they will not believe on the words of that freed prisoner, because they had been living in the cave in delusion since their childhood.

According to Plato, most of the people do not know the truth and they blindly follow the religious and social beliefs and rituals to be true. They are living in ignorance.

Once, Gautama Buddha was passing through a city. Many monks

were following him. Gautama Buddha's step was moving forward like a swan. His aura was divinely visible. Seeing Gautama Buddha, a person standing on the roadside went in front of Buddha and bowed down before him and asked him – Oh, divine man! Who are you? Are you an angel? Buddha said with a smile - no Dear. The man asked again - are you some Deva? Buddha again replied with smile - no Dear. Then the person asked- then who are you? Then Gautama Buddha said with compassion that now I have become Buddha, 'now I have come out of ignorance'.

Some people resort to lies, deceit, dishonesty and hypocrisy to accumulate wealth throughout their lives, but the end result of all their misdeeds go with them and after death the money earned by dishonest means remains in this world. The dead body turns into ashes when one dies. People also gradually forget that person. But because of the bad karmas he wanders in many lower realms in many rebirths. But due to ignorance he keeps doing so.

Saint Kabir warns such people, saying, " Ye nar tumne jhoothe janam gawayo, us jhooth ka koi ant na payo.' Meaning thereby, oh man! You have wasted your time and spoiled your life in falsehood and there is no end of that falsehood.

The 'Markandeya Purana' mentioned a great mother named Madalsa who used to give divine knowledge to her baby by singing Lori (Lullaby) in Sanskrit language. The meaning of the Lori sung in Sanskrit is as follows-

'Oh, Son! This world is changeable and dreamlike, so abandon the seduction of sleep, because you are pure Buddha and Niranjan(awaken). Oh, baby! You are pure consciousness, you have no name, you have just got this fictitious name, and your body is made up of five elements. Neither it is yours nor you belong to it, then why are you crying? All your senses which receive the qualities of virtue - are also made of five elements. You should not be gloomy by the degeneration of your tattered body. According to good karma this human body has been received, you should always be free from vices. Although all enjoyments are painful, however, those who are foolish consider them to be good and they are inclined for such enjoyment. But wise men are not bound by the attachment of the mind, they consider sensual enjoyment as means of suffering. Oh son! Stay away from the delusion of the world forever. The laughter of the women is merely a display of the bones of the mouth, the women's eyes which are said to be very beautiful, are also only the marrow and the glands of flesh. Therefore, the attraction for beautiful body is nothing but merely ignorance. Always keep your mind pure, my son. Keeping the conscience pure, conquer all six enemies like sexual desire, anger, greed, arrogance, attachment and envy. Oh son! Try to find the way through the right knowledge and by thinking about the impermanence of this world and lead your life according to the instructions of your soul.'

The civilization of Greece is very ancient. Greece has produced many great philosophers, historians and eminent persons in many fields, such as Socrates, Plato, Aristotle, Homer, Pythagoras, Archimedes, Euclid, Hippocrates, Herodotus and Alexander, etc.

During the reign of Alexander, there was a saint named Diogenes who lived on the bank of a river in Athens, the capital of Greece. He lived naked in his hut like Digambar Jain saints. His fame spread far and wide. People from far and wide used to come to see him. Once during the winter season, Diogenes was sitting outside his hut. At the same time Emperor Alexander came to meet Diogenes. Emperor Alexander told Saint Diogenes that – 'I am Emperor Alexander, I have come to meet you and to say that you live naked in this hut, this brings disgrace to my country. If you require anything, then speak to me, I am ready to fulfil your need.' Saint Diogenes smiled after hearing the words of Emperor Alexander and said that 'you please do me a favour, please move away from here and let the sun rays come.' Emperor Alexander was shocked by listening Diogenes. He thought that, 'this saint is fearless and he didn't pay any attention to me knowing that I am the emperor of this country.' Diogenes further said that 'you are hollow from inside and your craving is endless. You have not won yourself. First of all, conquer yourself only then you will be able to understand me. I do not need anything because I am full of joy from inside.'

Alexander began to think about Diogenes. He thought, this fakir is the real king, because he has conquered his mind and senses.

A few days after this incident, Alexander set out with his large army to conquer India. It is known that the Battle of Hydaspes was fought on the bank of Jhelum between Emperor Alexander and King Porus in 326 BC. Although Alexander was victorious in this battle but his army was badly damaged in this battle. Alexander's army was not inclined to advance further for conquest because it was afraid of the huge army of Maurya Emperor Chandragupta. For this reason, army of Alexander was reluctant to move across the Indus River. Alexander's health was also not in good condition. He decided to return to Greece by halting the conquest. His health worsened in the way and he eventually died in Alexandria, Iraq.

It is said that before death, Emperor Alexander called his commander and put his last three wishes before him.

1. That only my personal doctor would follow my coffin.
2. That gold, silver and gems should be scattered on the path through which the coffin will be taken, and
3. That my hands should be kept open outside the coffin.

Emperor Alexander made his final wish, keeping in mind that even his doctor could not save him from death. Even with so much money, he could not save his life from death. Leaving all this wealth behind, he is leaving this world empty-handed. Throughout his life, Alexander ran after his craving and conquered the lands which were won previously by so many people. While dying, Emperor Alexander remembered the sermon of Diogenes, that one who has conquered his mind and senses and craving, is the true king.

Actually, human beings remain unaware of the eternal truth of this world and the true nature of self. Man, lives in ignorance throughout his life. His mind is covered with infinite desires. Only a few yogis are able to detach themselves from the effects of Maya, otherwise an ordinary person is drowned into cravings till the death.

There lived a very wealthy merchant in a city. That merchant had four wives. The merchant loved his fourth wife the most. He loved his third wife a little less than the fourth and loved the second wife less than the third wife. The merchant had least love for his first wife. The merchant often ignored his first wife.

Once the merchant became very ill. His illness could not be cured and the doctors said that he is now guest in this world for a few days. The merchant summoned his dearest fourth wife and told her that, 'I am now departing from this world forever. I wish that you would also follow me. We both will leave this world together.' The fourth wife replied that she could only accompany him to the crematorium. The merchant was sad to hear this from his most beloved fourth wife. Then the merchant called his third wife and asked, "Will you go with me from this world?" The third wife said that after his death she would get married again. The merchant then called his second wife and asked the same question. Then the second wife said that she would accompany him to the crematorium. In the end, the merchant called his first wife whom he always ignored and asked her – 'would you join me in the last journey of my life.' Then the first wife of merchant accepted the proposal of her husband and said that she would give goodbye to this world with him.

The truth of human life has been explained through this metaphorical tale. Actually, the fourth wife is the body of a person whom he keeps attached throughout his life, but that body accompanies him up to the crematorium, where it finally merges with the five elements. The third wife is the wealth of the person, which goes in the hands of other members of the family after death. The second wife is near relatives or friends who go to the cremation to perform the last rites of the dead body and the first wife is the soul of the person who remains immortal even after leaving the body. But human beings never listen to the eternal soul and always ignore the voice of soul. The scriptures say that soul is indestructible, it adopts the new life of any creature according to the law of karma.

In fact, spiritual journey is self-introspection of life, the search for oneself. In this universe, all creatures, animals and nature are connected to each other. All beings take light of sun, air, water and continue their life cycle. Man is also one of the creatures of this infinite universe, but man does not understand the truth of this universe i.e., cosmic reality. His mind is so entangled in family, economic, social, political, communal and cultural aspects that he forgets himself. He does not understand the subtle mystery of nature and consciousness. Therefore, it is necessary for spiritual journey that the mind be withdrawn from the world. In other words, to detach oneself from worldly muddles, to get detached from attachment and hatred of the world and finally, to get engaged in meditation, vipassana and contemplation, that is, in the search of the God inside.

Prior to sowing seeds in the field, a farmer cleans the field. He weeds out the grasses and unwanted shrubs from the field and then he sows the seeds in the field. Even after the seed germination, the farmer continues to look after the crops. In the same way a spiritual seeker should eliminate the vices, such as sexual desires, anger, greed, ego, jealousy and other kinds of worldly attachments or hatred from the mind. The mind should be made clean. Once the mind becomes clean then the plants of peace, compassion, benevolence, joy, contentment, love and friendliness start growing on their own. A spiritual seeker should always keep an eye on the mind and senses so that they do not get entangled in the illusion of the world again. For this one should always remember God and study spiritual books like Bhagavad Gita, Upanishads, Yoga sutra, Buddhist and Jain literature or Gurugrantha Saheb.

Pranayama and the constant practice of meditation bring fundamental changes in life. The peace and happiness come in life through continuous devotion, meditation and by strictly following the moral code of conduct. Yoga, meditation or austerity are the means to cleanse the mind. Purity of mind is an essential condition for a spiritual seeker.

Saint Kabir says that-

'Tan ko jogi sab karai, man ko karai na koye
Sahjay sab sidhi paiye, jo man jogi hoye.'

People practice yoga for body, nobody does it for mind. One can be endowed with all powers, if one becomes yogi from the mind.

17
REALIZATION OF GOD AND SOUL (CONSCIOUSNESS)

God and soul have been discussed in almost all religions. It can be said that the existence of religions depends on the concept of God. People gather at the temples, mosques, churches and gurudwaras to worship God, but there are rare people who have got realisation of God or soul at these religious places. Actually, the realization of the God or the soul cannot be possible only through the study of religious books or joining the crowds at the places of worship. It is impossible to realize God or consciousness without meditating in solitude. It is important to make the mind detached from the outside world for meditation. God is omnipresent and cannot be imprisoned in any religious place. In fact, silence, serenity, solitude and detachment are path to realise God and soul.

In the Bhagavad Gita, Lord Krishna is telling Arjuna that,

'puruṣhaḥ sa paraḥ pārtha bhaktyā labhyas tvananyayā
yasyāntaḥ-sthāni bhūtāni yena sarvam idaṁ tatam.'

'Oh, Parth! that eternal unmanifested supreme God in whom all beings reside and by whom all this is pervaded, is attainable only through exclusive devotion.' (Bhagavad Gita - 8/22)

Again, Shri Krishna says –

'Na tu māṁ śhakyase draṣhṭum anenaiva sva-chakṣhuṣhā
Divyaṁ dadāmi te chakṣhuḥ paśhya me yogam aiśhwaram.'

'Oh, son of Kunti! You cannot see my cosmic form with these physical eyes of yours. You may see me through divine eye which I am granting to you. Behold my majestic opulence!' (Bhagavad Gita - 11/8)

It is clear through the aforesaid verses of Bhagavat Gita that God or soul cannot be realized by mind or through five senses, but it can be realised through continuous practice of deep meditation and quietness. The inner vision can only be awakened through meditation and one can realise God or consciousness in the state of samadhi when the mind and senses become empty, inactive.

There is a famous story of Shwetaketu in Chhandogya Upanishad. Shwetaketu, the son of sage Aruni Uddalaka, returned home after twelve years of education of Gurukula. The sage Uddalaka, after observing his son's behaviour, understood that Shwetaketu has acquired only bookish knowledge and his ego has still not gone. In fact, he has not yet acquired the right knowledge, because ego is the hallmark of ignorance. He thought that without knowledge of Brahman and soul, mere bookish knowledge is avidya (ignorance). True learning makes a person humble and intelligent, while ego is a sign of ignorance.

Sage Uddalaka called his son, Shwetaketu and asked him to sit with him. The sage asked his son – 'My dear son, do you know that, through which the unheard can be heard, the unseen can be seen and the unknown can be known?' Shwetketu was surprised to hear his father's words. He did not know anything about this subject. He said that his teachers have not given him such education.

Sage Uddalaka sat under a tree with Shwetaketu and picked up a little soil and said - Shwetaketu, when you know about the soil, then you can also know about all kinds of utensils or toys made of clay, since all these items have been made of soil and only their forms have been changed. When you know the gold, then you also know the different types of jewelleries made of gold. Only their forms have changed. In the same way, can you tell me that what is the basic element by which this whole world is made? Curious Shwetketu said, he didn't know.

Then sage Aruni Uddalaka said it is the consciousness from which the entire universe is made. Life cannot be imagined without it. There are only two eternal truths in this world, i.e., life and lifeless, in other word, living and non-living. The basic element is consciousness in all living beings. Even though the name and form are different of all living beings but there is consciousness in all living beings, like gold is basic element and all kinds of jewelleries made of gold, are having different shape and design.

Seeing the curiosity of Shvetketu in divine knowledge, the sage Uddalaka took him to a flower garden and said that after collecting the nectar from various flowers, the bees take it to their hive and make honey from it. Having seen that honey prepared from the nectar of different types of flowers, it would be difficult to say that this honey is made of which particular flower. Similarly, when a person understands that basic truth consciousness, then his complete illusion is removed. He understands that all beings have been created by that 'Brahman consciousness.' Once the knowledge of that ultimate truth is realized, all ignorance disappears itself. Just as rivers lose their existence after mixing in the ocean, similarly after death all creatures assimilate in the same Brahman consciousness and lose their independent identities. It is consciousness that connects everyone.

After listening to the above teachings, Shwetketu said - Father, how is this world with such a diversity been created by this consciousness?

The sage Uddalaka told his son Shwetaketu to bring a fruit of banyan tree from somewhere. When Shvetketu brought a fruit of banyan tree, Acharya Uddalaka told him to break the fruit and see what was inside? Shvetketu told his father Acharya Uddalaka that there were many small seeds in this fruit, which were so subtle that it was difficult to see. Then the sage Uddalaka said to Shwetaketu that 'the secret of a huge banyan tree is hidden in the subtle seed which you cannot easily see.' Just as this very subtle seed can produce a huge banyan tree with its various branches, in the same way the entire nature with such vastness and diversities has been created by the consciousness which we cannot see through the senses.

After this, Acharya Uddalaka asked Shvetaketu to bring water in a vessel and a pinch of salt. He asked Shwetketu to mix the pinch of salt in the water of the vessel and told him to slowly drink the water of the upper layer of the vessel, then the middle and finally the water of the lower layer of the vessel and tell him whether there is any difference in the water. After drinking the water of upper layer of vessel, then the water of middle layer and finally the water of bottom layer of vessel, Shwetaketu told that there is no difference. Then the sage Uddalaka said that as the salt is not visible even then each drop of water is salty, in the same way, Brahman consciousness is present in the whole universe.

When a person realizes the divine knowledge of Brahman consciousness through his inner vision, then he understands that all the beings in this world have been created by the same Brahman consciousness. There is only difference of name and form. Then all the illusions and ignorance of the person are eliminated and such enlightened person feels love and compassion for all creatures of the world, irrespective of colour, caste, creed, gender, language or other differences.

Saint Kabir puts the aforesaid fact in his own words, -

'Jaise tarubar beej mah, beej tarubare mahi
Kahe Kabir bichari ke, jag Brahm ke mahi.'

As there is seed, in the midst of tree and tree in the midst of seed,
Kabir says after thinking that this world is in the midst of God.
Saint Kabir again says -

"Jal me kumbh, kumbh me jal, bahar bhitar pani
Futa khumbh jal jal hi samana, yah tathya kathe gyani."

That is, as the pot made of soil when immersed in the ocean, is filled with water. There is water inside and outside of the pot in the ocean but still the water inside the pot (Kumbh) remains separate from the water outside. The reason for this separation is the form and shape of that pot. But as soon as the pot breaks down, water gets mixed up in the water of ocean and the differences disappear. In the same way this universe is like the cosmic ocean, the consciousness is all pervading like the water in ocean. All the creatures of universe are just like different pots in the oceans which are filled with consciousness. But due to the forms and colours of different living beings, there seems differences between them. But as soon as this body pot breaks, all the differences disappear. That is, when body made of five elements merges into the five elements of the nature after death and the consciousness of the body merges into Brahman consciousness.

Every human being has inherent natural qualities by which he may know about the subtle things of the nature but majority of people are not aware of their inherent powers and they waste their precious life only in the fulfilment of sensory desires. Nowadays, human mind is much entangled in the social, economic, political, communal and family matters. Unless a person's mind is made empty from the needless thoughts, the mind will not be suitable for the meditation and it is impossible to gain divine knowledge without meditation. That is why in every yoga practice, it has been emphasized repeatedly to clear the mind from unwanted thoughts. It is necessary to have detachment from the outside in order to go into oneself. It is necessary to engage the mind in the constant practice of meditation by withdrawing the mind and senses from the world and only then the insight vision would be awakened and only then it will be possible to understand the subject like Brahman and consciousness.

Saint Kabir further says -

'Ghunghat ke pat khol re, tohe piya milenge,
Ghat ghat me tere, sai basat hain, Katu bachan mat bol re,
Dhan -Pad ka garb Na kije, jhutha inaka mol re,

Jag yatan se rang mahal me, piya payo anamol re,
Sune mandir me diya jala ke, aasan se mat dol re,
Kahat 'Kabir' suno bhai sadhu, Anhad bajat dol re.'

Saint Kabir advised the human beings to remove the veil of ignorance which has covered the mind like the veil of a face. Only then you will see God, otherwise you will die in the darkness of ignorance. God is inside all beings as consciousness, so avoid lose tongue and behave properly with everyone. He further said that you should not have arrogance of wealth and position because all are temporary and perishable. Your body which is also an earthen pot and it is perishable. Just stabilize your mind and body and meditate and experience that formless consciousness-Brahman in the state of samadhi. Listen carefully to the sound coming from your heart, that is, 'anhad nad'.

It is said in the 'Shvetashvatara Upanishad' that-

"Tileṣu tailaṃ dadhanīva sarpir āpaḥ srotaḥsv araṇīṣu cāgniḥ,
Evam ātmā ātmani gṛhyate 'sau satyenainaṃ tapasā yo 'nupaśyati."

Like the oil is in the sesame seeds or butter in the cream, water in the river beds or fire in the wooden sticks, so is the soul hidden in oneself, which can be grasped through truthfulness and austerity. (Shvetashvatara Upanishad - 1/15)

There has been misconception among the people regarding actual place of God. After all, how will God be realized? Yes, God is omnipresent. He is in every living being. He is non-dual. That formless Brahman is omnipresent. The only way to know him is to know oneself.

Sant Kabir says -

'Jaise til me tel hai jyo chakmak me Aag,
Tera sai tujhh me hai Jan sake to Jan.'

Sant Kabir says that, just as there is oil in sesame, fire in flint, in the same way your God is within you. You have to know how oil can

be taken out of sesame, fire from flint and how God can be realised within one's self.

Actually, the human mind is the real source through which any mystery can be known. But if the mind is polluted and disturbed, then nothing can be known. Just like the stones inside the clean and calm pond water are visible, similarly if the mind is clean, without disorder, then by continuous effort of meditation, we can realise our inner God.

Actually, God is neither in a temple, mosque, church or gurudwara nor in any pilgrimage or shrine. Again, Sant Kabir says –

'Moko kahan dhundhe re bande,
Mai to tere pas me
Na tirath, Na Murat me
Na mandir, Na masjid me
Na kaba, kailash me
Mai to tere pas re bande
Mai to tere pas me.'

The meaning of aforesaid couplet is that 'where are you searching me? I am within you. I am neither in temple nor in masque, I am neither at pilgrimage nor in idols, I am neither at Kaaba nor at Kailash. Oh man! I am within you.'

Man dies one day living in ignorance. He does not know that he himself is the form of Brahman. Chhandogya Upanishad has called 'Tat Tvam Asi' or 'Tattvamasi' which means that God is within you, in me and in everyone. Brihadarankya Upanishad called 'Aham Brahmasmi,' i.e. 'I am brahman'. The realization of one's Brahman form can be done only in the state of deep meditation, that is, in the state of samadhi. However, the Subconscious of human mind is filled with sexual desire and infinite cravings. The mind is full of filth. Due to these reasons man is not able to know about his Brahman form.

Sant Kabir further says -

'Aatm chinhe parmatm chinhe sant kahawe soi
Yah bhed kaya se nayara, jane birla koi.'

That is, one is a real saint who has realized self, the consciousness. He realises the God, but there are very few persons in the world who understand that there is consciousness within their body which is part of God.

Saint Kabir again says –

'Mai janu Hari door hai, Hari hirday bharpoor
Manush dhudhai bahira, niaray hokar door'.

People think that God is far away but God is in the heart of every being. People search God outside, but he is within oneself but seems far away.

It is important to discuss this story on consciousness. Once upon a time, a king rode on his horse and went out alone to hunt in the forest. He wandered around in the forest, but could not find any prey. The forest was very large and dense. While wandering in the forest king forgot the way to his palace. Meanwhile, he got very thirsty and started wandering in search of water. After a while, he saw a pond. He tied his horse to a tree. He saw a hut in front of the pond. A Mahatma was in deep meditation under a tree in front of that hut. The king thought that after drinking the water from the pond and bathing in it, it would be appropriate to see Mahatma. The king first drank the water of the pond. The water of the pond was very clean and sweet. After drinking the water, the king's mind became calm and happy. He then put off his clothes and kept them on the bank of the pond and started bathing in the pond. While bathing, his mind became calm and clean and he started meditating. Gradually he got absorbed in samadhi. In the state of samadhi, he realized the supreme consciousness. He felt that God is present within him.

Meanwhile, Mahatma got up from meditation and started walking, he saw a person in samadhi while standing in the pond. The Mahatma, through his divine vision, came to know everything about that king.

After some time, the king woke up from samadhi. He came out of the pond, wore his clothes and then bowed down before Mahatma.

The king said to Mahatma – 'Oh Mahatma! Is there any miraculous divine power in this pond?' After drinking the water of this pond, my mind became calm, serene and blissful and while bathing, I experienced wonderful divinity which I am unable to explain in words.'

The Mahatma said that, 'this pond is very holy by the way. In this pond, I go into samadhi every day, due to which its waves have also been divinely energised. But the biggest reason is that you were sure to have realisation of the supreme consciousness in this pond. Oh king! You were a monk in previous life and did penance in this forest to attain salvation. But in that life, you did not get salvation. You have realization of supreme consciousness in this pond as a result of your previous accumulated good deeds.'

The Mahatma further said that – 'Oh king! This life is full of mysteries. Many events occur in human life, which is not understood by the common man. Only a few knowledgeable seers understand these esoteric mysteries through their insight. Many pleasant and tragic events in life occur due to the previous karmas. You have got this divine experience because of the austerity of your previous life. Oh king! You should do your karma in the right direction so that you may get a pleasant result. You should not kill any creature for hunting otherwise it can ruin your good karma.' The king took pledge before Mahatma to practice non-violence and returned to his palace. He remained engaged in the selfless service like a monk.

18
LAW OF KARMA

Saint Kabir says –

'Karna tha so nahi kiya ab Kari kyo pachhtay
Ropa ped babul ka Aam kaha se khay.'

i.e., you did not do what ought to have been done and now you are repenting. If you plant acacia tree (a thorny tree usually found in the desert area), then how can you get mango?

Saint Tulsi Das says-

'Karma Pradhan Vishwa Rachi Rakha
Jo jas karni tas phal chakha.'

Means, in this world, karma is important. Whatever one does, gets the fruit of that action.

Saints and Mahatmas have always advised the people to do good action and stay away from bad deeds. The karma makes human life beautiful and also ruin the life. Only the quality of karma is important. The karma which is for the personal gain but is harmful to another person or any other creature, cannot be said to be a good karma, but such a deed is a misdeed. The unrighteous karma eventually brings bad consequences for the one who has done it. Saint Tulsi Das says –'Parhit saris dharm nahi bhai, parpeeda sam nahi adhmai.' Means, there is no religion greater than doing good to others, and there is no unrighteousness as to harm others. Theft, robbery, violence, falsehood, fraud, bribery, drug trafficking or other misdeeds may bring immediate economic gains, but such bad deeds will eventually bring bad results. The law of karma is unalterable and it is a natural law. A man reaps what he sows. If man will plant a mango tree, he will get mango. But if he plants thorny tree, he will get only thorns.

In Hindu, Jain, Buddhist and Sikh philosophies, the law of karma has been described in great detail. There is a consensus in all religious philosophies that human beings should do their karma consciously. According to the rules of karma, even the good and bad intentions bring good and bad results.

A human being performs his karma in three ways, that is, he performs his actions through body, mind and speech. Each karma performed through the mind, body and speech bring similar reaction or result. According to the law of karma, every karma of a human being brings result in the same proportion. The story of Raja Dasharatha and Shravan Kumar is based on this karma.

Shravan Kumar was taking his blind and old parents by Kawad (Two baskets fastened to a bamboo stick which is carried on shoulder) for pilgrimage. While passing through a forest, Shravan Kumar's parents felt very thirsty. Shravan left his parents in a safe place and went to fetch water for them in an earthen pot. The king of Ajodhya, King Dasharatha was also in that forest for hunting. When Shravan Kumar was filling water in the pitcher, King Dasharatha got confused on hearing the sound of water filling in the pitcher and thought it to be the sound of an animal and he suddenly fired a spraining arrow on it. That arrow pierced the chest of Shravan Kumar. King Dasharatha realized his mistake on hearing Shravan's scream and ran to the spot. He saw a young man injured by his arrow. In the injured state, Shravan Kumar gave his introduction and then requested the king to take the pitcher filled with water to his thirsty parents. Having said that Shravan died. King Dasharatha felt very sad about this incident. He went to Shravan's parents with the pitcher filled with water. Then the blind parents, considering the sound of King Dasharatha feet as the sound of their son Shravan's feet, said, "Son Shravan, why did you delay in bringing water?" Then King Dasharatha narrated everything to Shravan Kumar's parents. After hearing this depressing news, the old and blind parents began to mourn and sadly said, 'oh king! Someday you will also mourn for your son in the same way as we are mourning for our son.' It is known that King Dasharatha began to remain unhappy after his son's exile. At the last moment, King Dasharatha became frustrated for his lovely son Rama, and ultimately died in acute pain.

The mind plays an important role in the accomplishment of the karma. First, the thought or feelings come to the mind and then the mind orders other senses to implement those thoughts. Therefore, every person should try to keep the mind clean by yoga, meditation or vipassana. The mind motivates a man to commit sin or do virtuous deed. Negative emotions like violence, sexuality, anger, greed, egoism and hatred come in the mind and encourage a man to commit sinful deeds. Sin disturbs the peace and happiness of the doer and also spoils the fruit of the karma. Lord Buddha used to say that the mind is the leader of all good and bad deeds, so keep an eye on your own mind through Vipassana meditation method. When positive feelings come in the mind, then the feelings of love, compassion, benevolence come which creates a feeling of peace and happiness. The actions done with these feelings also have good results.

There are three types of Karma: -

1. Sanchit Karma - Sanchit karma is the accumulated sum of good and bad deeds of this life and past lives.
2. The Prarabhda karma or destiny karma- It is the good or bad karma that a person had done in his previous life and its fruit he is enjoying in this life. Like someone born in a rich family, becomes millionaire even though he did not make any effort to earn that property, rather he is reaping the destiny of previous deed, or one who has been dragged in the false cases or trouble even after his non-involvement in such misdeeds due to previous bad karma.

3. Aagam or Kriyamana Karma - The person is currently performing Karma, but its result is yet to come.

In Chapter 6 of the 'Anushasna Parva' of Mahabharata, Bhishma Pitamah while imparting knowledge to Yudhishthira says that - Oh Yudhishthira! Just as crops cannot be produced without sowing seeds in the field, in the same way, destiny or luck is also not made without effort. The quality of labour is the seed. The destiny is the crop. Grain is produced only by the combination of field and seed.

A man who performs a deed for self bears the fruits of his good or bad deeds. An auspicious action brings happiness and sorrow comes from performing sinful actions. The work done by us, give rise to the fruits. The fruit of karma without doing any karma is impossible. A laborious person gets the fruits of karma; but the lazy suffers from the sorrow.

Every person has to bear the fruits of good and bad karma done by him in this birth or forthcoming life. The results of good or bad actions come immediately in some cases and in some cases comes later. If a person always speaks lies then the result is that people gradually stop relying on him or if a person drinks too much alcohol, his kidney gets damaged. The result of such action comes immediately. In some cases, it is seen that misfortune happens with noble persons. There was an incident of Lord Buddha's time that an Arhat became blind in his middle age. Due to blindness, he had to suffer a lot in performing his activities. A person is called Arhat who has overcome all his human weaknesses and attained nirvana. One Buddhist monk asked Lord Buddha, Oh Buddha! Why did the blindness happen to that arhat? Then Lord Buddha meditated and with his divine vision he found out that the Arhat was a physician in his previous life and he deliberately spoiled the eyes of a woman, because she refused to do his household works. When the woman had problem in her eyes, she came to get her treatment from that doctor. The doctor had intentionally spoiled her eyes by giving her the wrong medicine. That is why he has to be blind in this birth.

There is a legend of Mahabharata. In the fierce battle of Mahabharata, Bhishma Pitamah was badly wounded by the arrows of great archer Arjuna and his back was completely filled with the arrows shot by Arjuna. He fell down from his chariot in injured state. But instead of falling on the ground, his body was hung over the arrows and the entire arrows appeared as a bed of arrows which was very painful for Bhishma Pitamah. Devavrata Bhishma had got a boon from his father king Shantanu that he would die when he wished. He was enduring pain while lying on the bed of arrows. By now, the battle of Kurukshetra was almost over. Shri Krishna and Arjuna went to see Bhishma Pitamah. Bhishma Pitamah requested Arjuna that he needed a pillow so that he could rest. Arjuna made a pillow for Bhishma Pitamah by his arrows.

Meanwhile, Bhishma Pitamah told Shri Krishna that – 'Oh Keshav! You are omniscient. I remember my own story of the last seventeen lives. I had never done any sinful act, yet why am I suffering from this unbearable pain? Why is this happening to me? Please tell me.' Then Shri Krishna said – 'Oh Bhishma Bhitamah! You only remember the story of the last seventeen births, but you do not remember anything of your 18th birth. In that birth, when you were a prince, you were riding on your horse and passing through a forest. On the way you found a snake resting on the side of the road. You picked up that snake with your arrow without any reason, and threw it so forcefully that the poor snake fell on a thorny plant and the thorns of plant pierced its body. Its family members mourned a lot. After suffering for many days, the snake lost its life. That serpent was upset and cursed you.' The snake said 'may you suffer from the same pain from which I am suffering!'

Shri Krishna further said that, Oh Bhishma Pitamah! The sinful act you had done in the 18th birth, had not yet fructified, because till now, your accumulated good karmas were more than the sinful karma. Due to accumulated good deeds, your sin was covered. But when Dushasana tried to denude Dravapadi in the court of Duryodhana and she was pleading for help to save her prestige, you were also watching everything. At that time, your duty was to protest against that injustice. But even after watching everything, you remained silent and indirectly you had supported the unrighteousness. At that time your accumulated good karmas were finished and the previous accumulated sin karma was to come out and finally it came. As that snake was lying on the bed of thorns for many days and was suffering from severe pain, similarly you too are lying on the bed of thorns and waiting to die.

'Oh, son of Ganga! You also know very well that you had committed unrighteousness with Amba which was a cause for your destruction. You know very well that you had kidnapped the three daughters of the king of Kashi, for the marriage of your brother Vichitravirya. Ambika and Ambalika got married to Vichitravirya. But you disrespected Amba by not marrying her. You probably know that Amba took many births and did severe penance to take avenge of that insult. In the end, by doing penance to Lord Shiva, she obtained the blessing and finally she was born as Shikhandi in the house of King Drupada. Shikhandi became the cause for your destruction. Shikhandi is the reincarnation of Amba who has caused your destruction.'

Every human has to bear the fruits of his good and bad deeds in this life or upcoming life. This is the law of karma. The law of karma is so strong that till date no one could escape from it. Due to sin karma, human being take birth in low realms like insects. This is why Sant Kabir has cautioned the people:

'Karam gati tare nahi tari.
Muni Vasishth Se Pandit Gyaanee Sodh Ke Lagan Dharee.
Sita Haran Maran Dasharath Ke Van mein Vipati Paree
Paandav Jinake Krishn Saarathee Tin Par Vipati Paree
Duryodhay ke Garv Ghatao, Yadukul Nash Kari
Kahat Kabeer Suno Bhaee Saadho Honee Hoy ke Rahee.'

That is, the result of karma definitely happens, it cannot be avoided. Knowledgeable pundit like Muni Vasishta had made horoscope of Shri Rama after much research, yet Rama had to suffer in the jungle. His wife Sita was kidnapped and in the meantime his father king Dasharatha also died. Similarly, Pandavas had to suffer a lot. Duryodhana's arrogance vanished and the dynasty of 'Yadu' was also destroyed. All this happened due to the law of karma.

It is said that after the death of King Dasharatha, Bharata went to meet his dearest brother Shri Rama in the forest and urged him – 'Oh my dear brother! You now return to Ajodhya. Father is no more. All the residents of Awadh and family members are waiting for you.' Then Lord Shri Rama while explaining to his younger brother Bharata, said – 'Oh my dear brother Bharata! Every man has to bear the fruits of his karma done in his past lives in many births. This exile is also on the account of the deeds of my previous lives. Therefore, brother Bharata, do not be sad and continue to serve the subjects living like a monk.' There are many unsolved mysteries in life, which only a few Mahatmas can understand by their divine knowledge and ordinary people do not know anything about the mystery of life. Therefore, they do not understand the distinction between karma, detached karma and sinful karma and push their lives to darkness.

19
THE REALITY OF THE PRINCIPLE OF REBIRTH

Both birth and death are very important days in a human being's life. This is why it is the practice to celebrate birthday and death anniversary. The life of every creature on this earth is limited. All beings in this world are mortal. Only God is imperishable, everlasting and unchangeable. All other living beings are temporary, perishable and changeable.

Hindus, Jains, Buddhists and Sikhs consider the human body to be perishable and the charioteer of that body, i.e., the soul (consciousness) that keeps that body alive is imperishable. This soul abandons one body and takes another body, just as a person renounces his old clothes and wears a new clothes. (Bhagavad Gita - 2/22). Thus Atman (consciousness) is eternal. 'Ishwar Ansh Jiva Avinashi Chetan Amal Sahaj Sukhrasi.'i.e., Atman is the part of God and source of happiness. So, the body dies, but the soul is immortal. But it is not necessary that the soul after leaving the body of a man re-enters a human body. According to the law of karma, the soul of human being can be reborn in any other species. According to Hindu religion, there are 8.4 million realms of living beings. There can be rebirth in any realm. According to Buddhist religion, after death, a person may reborn in any of the six realms, namely, Deva, Asura, Human, Animal, Phantom or may go to hell, according to good and bad karma.

Thus, the soul takes any form, as the water transforms into snow, vapour, cloud and rain, but their basic form is water. In the same way, the soul can adopt any form of human being, animal, bird, insect or fly, according to the karma of previous life.

It is to be noted here that a zygote (cell) is formed by the union of sperm and egg and the same cell gradually undergoes many processes. Within thirty to forty days a human infant starts taking shape, and in the same period the soul enters the body. Gradually the organs of the baby go on developing in the mother's womb. In the womb of the mother, the body of baby is formed by the physical elements through food, water, air and other natural elements taken by the mother. Genetic science holds that the child inherits the traits from the parent's family tree because of the combination of sperm and egg. It can be detected by DNA test.

When the soul enters into the child's body in the mother's womb, the mind (Chita) of the previous body goes with the soul in the same way as the wind picks up the smell from the place of smell and carries it away with it. (Bhagavad Gita-15/8). This is to be noted that innumerable memories of many past lives remain in dormant state in the subconscious of human mind, just like the memory of computer software. The subconscious mind is like a pen drive which keeps all the forgotten memories alive for many births, which can be known through the technique of hypnosis.

Nowadays hypnosis is used by psychiatrists to treat some mental illnesses. Sometimes a person gets nervous by seeing or hearing about a particular person, object or place or sometime one has recurrent scary dreams of the same nature. Then the psychiatrists try to find out the main reason of such type of mental restlessness, nervousness, or scary dreams which come up again and again. In such a situation, psychiatrists use some special technique to find out past memories of the patient from the subconscious mind through hypnosis. He tries to know whether any bad incident occurred with the mentally sick person. Sometimes, in some cases some incidents occurred in the previous life of the patient. The method followed by psychiatrists is called, past life regression therapy.

A similar case is mentioned by the famous American Psychotherapist, Dr. Brian Weiss in his famous book - 'Many Lives and Many Masters', (Many Lives and Many Souls).

The true story in the said book is that of a young woman named Catherine, who was suffering from nightmares and brain restlessness. She was often depressed in her office and was hesitant to tell anyone about her sadness. Once a colleague in the office asked her about the reason for her sadness. Then Catherine told him about her mental condition. The colleague advised Catherine that she should consult a good psychiatrist and suggested the name of Dr. Brian Weise. Although Catherine did not want to go to a psychiatrist, she was forced by her mental condition to talk about her illness to Dr. Brian Weiss. Dr. Weiss tried to cure Catherine with traditional medicines but he could not cure her illness. After this, Dr. Brian used the technique of hypnosis to know about the past life of Catherine from her own mouth. The revelations from Catherine's mouth were truly astonishing for Dr. Weiss. Dr. Weiss used the hypnosis technique several time on Catherine to find out more information of her past lives and after conducting an independent investigation of all those events, he became absolutely convinced. Actually, in the beginning Doctor Weiss did not believe in rebirth. For this reason, an investigation into the disclosure of Catherine was necessary. During the revelations of previous life, Catherine narrated in many languages some very old incidents that happened in several other countries. Dr. Brian Weiss succeeded in curing Catherine's illness by uncovering the several layers of Catherine's previous lives.

Prior to this, there is another book of 1966 titled "Twenty Cases suggestive of Reincarnation." The book was written by Dr Ian Stevenson, a Canadian native and professor in the Department of Psychiatry of the University of Virginia, USA. Apart from this book, Dr. Stevenson wrote several other books which have been published in many languages. In all these books, he has supported the principle of rebirth. An US neurosurgeon, Dr. Eben Alexander has also described the rebirth, as true.

In the modern era, psychiatrists use the technique of past life regression to cure mental patients, but Lord Buddha and Lord Mahavira used this method for the practice of asceticism. At that time this method was called 'Jati remembrance.' Jati remembrance was a method of deep meditation by which a person came to know about his previous lives. It is said that Lord Buddha knew about his many past lives.

Lord Buddha believed that no person can be a complete monk until he understands this life cycle well. Human life is just a repetition. In every life, a man keeps walking on the same route. For example, marrying, producing children, building house, making money through lies and dishonesty and then leaving the world and coming back to the world and doing the same things again. Lord Buddha used to tell the monks that through deep meditation one could know about the past life. A man can also get out of this life cycle by attainment of nirvana. Lord Buddha believed that when a monk comes to know about his past life, he becomes disillusioned from this world and he starts concentrating for the attainment of nirvana. This message of Lord Buddha was propagated by Emperor Ashoka and the cycle of human life has been explained through the Ashoka Chakra. It is to be known that there are twenty-four spokes in the Ashoka Chakra. The twelve spokes represent causes for the human sufferings and other twelve spokes represent the remedies for the human sufferings.

It is said that when a person is in the dying state, he begins to feel the souls of his dead near relatives or neighbours. In such a situation soul of dying person gets attached to this world and wants to come back to this world. Such situation is a hindrance in the liberation. For this reason, a dying person is advised to meditate on God or listen to the text of the Bhagavad Gita or other sacred book so that his soul can be liberated.

In Tibet, a system was developed years ago for the emancipation of a dying person, which is still in vogue. This method is called 'Bardo Thodol'. The text of the 'book Bardo Thodol' is read out before a dying person. The Bardo Thodol text was presumably composed around the eighth century. Its author was Acharya Padma Sambhava, who was a Tibetan and was a professor of Buddhist philosophy at the ancient Nalanda University in Bihar.

In those days, people were often fearful of death due to the recurrent occurrence of natural disasters in Tibet. Acharya Padma Sambhav composed this book to remove the fear of death from the mind of people and to liberate people from the cycle of life. He had conveyed to the people through this book that the end of this body is just the end of a cycle of the infinite life cycles, like the flame of a lamp is a collection of infinite subtle flames. After the end of a subtle flame, the cycles of countless subtle flames come on one by one. In this way, the chain of infinite flame keeps going. In the same way the life cycle of human beings also keeps on going. The end of the life cycle means end of flames, i.e., nirvana or the attainment of salvation. For this reason, fear of death is just ignorance. Acharya Padma Sambhav said that according to the karma, the man's life cycle goes on forever.

'Bardo Thodol' is a method of hearing meditation. Some people read this book before a dying person and his/her attention is drawn to listen to it carefully. Through this a dying person is told that he will take another body according to his karma and he will again come back on this earth and again he will suffer. Therefore, he should remember Buddha or other Bodhisattvas for his salvation and go with them keeping in mind their illumination so that he may find the path for salvation. It is to be mentioned here that Bodhisattvas are said to be those persons who have attained ten Paramitas namely, (Mudita, Vimala, Deepti, Archishmati, Sudurjaya, Abhimukhi, Doorangama, Achal, Sadhumati and Dhamma-Megha) in their lifetime. They are all superior divine qualities.

Bardo Thodol system has been designed to guide the dying person so that he may get right direction for liberation. But some experts believe that, the same thoughts would come in the mind at the last moment, which the person has been accumulating in his mind till now. This is what Lord Shri Krishna has said in Bhagavad Gita that, 'oh son of Kunti! Whatever thoughts prominently dominate a person's mind at the moment of death determine his or her next birth.' Salvation cannot be attained merely by meditating on God at the time of death but it should be remembered that whatever vision, thinking and action remains in the whole life of a person, the same thoughts keep coming to the mind at time of death. (Bhagavad Gita - 8/6,7) In this way, the entire life vision of a person has to be good, otherwise it would prove as ritual and for this reason, Lord Buddha, Lord Mahavira and Maharishi Patanjali always used to remind people to keep an eye on the mind, deeds and words and do not let any negative feelings arise in the mind and follow the Yama and Niyama throughout life. Otherwise, the corrupt mind will be a hindrance in the path of liberation. In the Bhagavad Gita, Lord Krishna has shown the path of enlightenment, devotion and unattached karma for salvation. Upanishads advised to stay away from ignorance forever. In short, Indian religions believe that the attainment of vidya by removing the five tribulations (punch klesha, viz. sexual desire, anger, ego, greed and hatred) from the mind is very important for salvation.

People have been believing in the theory of rebirth since ancient times. People believed in reincarnation in ancient Egypt, Greece and ancient China. The famous philosophers of Greece like Pythagoras, Socrates, Plato, and Lao of China believed in the theory of rebirth. Hindus, Jains, Buddhists and Sikhs of Indian religions believe completely in rebirth. Some sects of Christianity also believe in rebirth, but Islam does not believe in rebirth, but some sects of Sufi believe in rebirth. There is dearth of deep philosophical research in Islam, while Indian religions have gone very deep since early days and unearthed the truth. In fact, Indian religions are the outcome of inside knowledge gained through continuous research, investigation and meditation. The sages of the Upanishads and Maharishi used to go to the forests and acquired wisdom over the years through deep meditation and transferred it to their disciples. Whatever has been written in the authentic texts like Bhagavad Gita, Patanjali Yoga Sutras, Buddhist and Jain literatures, were written after much research. For this reason, it would be foolish to mistrust these texts.

Maharishi Patanjali in his Yoga Sutra has given some methods to check the truth of any concept of any subject in Sutra (1/7) of Yoga Sutra, on the basis of which the truth of any subject can be ascertained.

1. Direct knowledge - The information or perception which is known through the five senses by seeing, hearing, touching, tasting or sensing is called direct knowledge but knowledge of the soul (consciousness) is not possible with these senses. This knowledge is not tangible knowledge. Spiritual knowledge cannot be understood by the senses and the principle of rebirth is based on the concept of immortality of soul.
2. Knowledge by inference- Knowledge is also attained by inference. If smoke is appearing, it means fire is burning somewhere. If the road or land is wet all around it means that there must have been rain. The soul cannot be known on the basis of conjecture. It would be foolish to understand rebirth on the basis of presumption.
3. Agama knowledge - the knowledge that can be acquired by any authentic scripture. Hindu, Jain and Sikh scriptures believe in the immortality of soul and rebirth, while Buddhism considers science or consciousness as eternal and believes fully in rebirth.
4. Pramanani (proof) - Proof knowledge is the knowledge of self-realisation. This self-realization can be attained in the state of deep meditation. It is only in the state of samadhi that one realizes the soul (consciousness). The soul or consciousness is the basic element of life, without it the body is lifeless. One who has understood that he is not only a body made of senses (five senses of knowing and sensing, five senses of physical work and mind) but he is a soul (consciousness), then he has understood everything. Then he will not doubt on the principle of rebirth. But to know it, deep meditation is required.

All Indian religions have put emphasis on the eternal nature of the soul (consciousness) and rebirth and warned the people to be careful of their conducts and karma because everything is dependent on the karma and there is no intervention of God in karma. The knowledge given by Lord Shri Krishna in Bhagwat Gita, the teachings of the great sages like Lord Buddha, Lord Mahavira, Saint Kabir and Guru Nanak have repeatedly cautioned people to be conscious of their deeds. They have advised the people that if their deeds will be like devas, then they will go into devaloka,(realm of devas) but if their deeds will be like animals then they will be born as an animal and if their deeds will be like devils, then they will go into the phantom loka. Your future is determined according to your karma and there will be no intervention of God in it.

But today people are wandering in the darkness of ignorance, forgetting the scriptures and the teachings of great seers. Their deeds have become worse than animals. They have been entrapped into unethical competition for accumulating wealth and power and are deeply indulged in sense craving. Perhaps they have forgotten the end of Alexander and Genghis Khan who came to this earth, conquered many wars but left this earth empty handed. They took with them only cravings, hatred, mental restlessness and sensual lust. Today, people are also unfamiliar with event of history. Diogenes, a fakir despised Alexander's deeds and did not value him but some ignorant people consider Alexander as great who fought many battles, killing innumerable innocent people.

Lord Buddha used to remind the monks that they should understand the impermanence of the nature and lead their life being detached from the world and move forward to the goal of attaining nirvana. That is why saints and sages did not feel fascinated by their body, considering the impermanence of this body. They believed in immortality of the soul, and had no fear of death.

Baba Gorakhnath says –

'Maro he yogi, Maran hai bada mitha
Us marani maro jis marani Gorakh Mari dithha.'

Baba Gorakhnath said that dying is too sweet and blissful, there is nothing to fear. You should live like a yogi and die as Gorakhnath had experienced this blissful moment of death.

Saint Kabir says –

'Jis marani se jag dare, mero man anand
Kab mariho kab bhetiyo purn Parmanand.'

That the death of which people are generally afraid, his heart gets delighted on hearing it and he start thinking when will he get that moment of ecstasy.

20
DIVINE KNOWLEDGE TO KING PARIKSHIT

'Oh King Parikshit! The aim of all the scriptures is to remove the ignorance from the mind of the people and to tell them about the path of salvation, that is, to show them the path of liberation from the cycle of birth and death. The biggest obstacle in the path of liberation, i.e., salvation is avidya i.e., ignorance. Not knowing self-knowledge or divine knowledge is avidya. Avidya is called Maya. Maya is the cause of bondage and when the cloud of delusion is removed, then only divinity is attained. Oh king! Try to get divine knowledge for getting rid of Maya (ignorance), only then you will get freedom from the cycle of birth and death. Considering this body to be mortal, detach your mind and senses from this momentary and ephemeral world and concentrate yourself to get the glimpse of ultimate truth, i.e., eternal God. Experience the God particle, the soul (consciousness) through constant meditation and devotion. Gradually you will begin to realise supreme consciousness. Bhakti yoga and Gyan yoga are two paths to get divine knowledge in which the path of devotion is easy. So, do not waste your time and devote yourself to Bhagavata Bhajan.'

The aforesaid teaching was imparted to king Parikshit, the grandson of Arjuna and son of Abhimanyu by ascetic Shukdeva Ji. Only few days were left for king Parikshit in this world. Shukdevji was a great saint of the Mahabharata period. He was the son of Ved Vyas ji. He had gone to the forest to do penance since the childhood. He narrated the Bhagavata tale to King Parikshit and showed the path of salvation which is described in the Bhagavata Purana.

The Kauravas were completely destroyed by the battle of Mahabharata. Yudhishthira, the eldest brother of the Pandava became the king of Hastinapur. But despite the victory, the Pandavas were depressed due to the death of their kith and kin, Guru Dronacharya and Pitamah Bhishma etc. They were not interested in the governance. They repeatedly remembered their cousins, Guru, Pitamah and brother Karna. They used to remember the loving relationships of the childhood days which made them sad. They thought that the fierce battle had happened due to disharmony and arrogance which had ruined everything.

The Pandavas finally handed over the throne of Hastinapur to Parikshit, son of Abhimanyu and grandson of Arjuna and went to Himalayas to do penance and atonement. King Parikshit proved to be a worthy and benevolent king.

Now the time has changed and after the Satyuga, Treta and Dwapara, the time of Kalyuga, (the age of ignorance) has come. Lord Krishna had foretold the evils of the Kalyuga to the Pandavas and said that in Kalyuga, the decline of religion and morality will take place. Only the true devotee of God can be saved from the brunt of Kalyuga.

Saint Soot ji narrated the story of devotion of Shri Krishna to the hermits and said that he had heard this story from the great seer Shukdeva Ji. The Bhagavata story narrated by Mahatma Shukdev to Maharaja Parikshit is described in the Bhagavata Purana.

Once king Parikshit set out towards the forest to hunt. He saw a demon-like person near the forest, who was unnecessarily beating a cow and a bull. King Parikshit scolded that person and asked him why he did the audacity to beat the cow and the bull, the symbol of religion in the kingdom of King Parikshit. He further said that he will get severe punishment for this mischief. King Parikshit proceeded to punish that demon like person but he fell down at the feet of King Parikshit and begged for mercy and requested for his shelter in his kingdom.

Then King Parikshit said 'okay, I am forgiving you, but tell me why you were doing such mischief? Then the person who looked like a demon said - Oh compassionate king Parikshit! I am Kalyuga. Then the King Parikshit said what the need of Kalyuga in his kingdom is? The kingdom is run according to righteousness. Get away from here soon. Then Kalyuga told king Parikshit that - Oh king! The Satyug, Treta and Dwapara age has now ended and now arrival of Kalyuga is according to the cycle of time which is a natural process. Ignoring the time cycle is the violation of the law of nature. After listening carefully to Kalyuga, King Parikshit said it is right that man should not interfere in the rules of nature, but you will not get freedom to roam freely in my kingdom. Since you have sought refuge in my kingdom, I will give you only four places where you can live. You can live in brothels, casinos, alehouse (bar) and slaughterhouses. These four places are places of unrighteousness, so you can stay there. After this, Kalyuga urged King Parikshit and said that, oh compassionate King Parikshit! The above four places have been infamous since time immemorial, so please give me some other place besides those. Then King Parikshit said that okay - you can live in gold also, because gold is the main reason for greed and attachment. Kalyuga was very happy with King Parikshit and expressed thanks to King Parikshit and then he disappeared. Now Kalyuga took his subtle form, sat in the golden crown of King Parikshit and started corrupting the mind of the King.

The Kalyuga was hiding in the golden crown of King Parikshit. In the meantime, the king was very much tired and thirsty due to running after hunting. In search of water, King Parikshit reached the ashram of Shamik Rishi. At that time, Shamik Rishi was sitting in samadhi. King Parikshit said with a loud voice that - I am King Parikshit, I am very thirsty. Since Shamik Rishi was in the Samadhi, he could not listen to the king's words. Kalyuga, seating in the crown of King Parikshit started instigating him against the Shamik Rishi, telling him that he is a hypocritical monk, pretending to be in meditation. Kalyuga was instigating the rage of the king and provoking the king to kill the sage, but the inherent nature of the king was preventing him from committing such a sinful act. After getting no water, the king took a dead snake from his arrow and wrapped it in the neck of Shamik Rishi and left the ashram.

Thereafter some of the children of the ashram reported this incident to Shringi, the son of sage Shamik Rishi who was taking bath in the river at that time. Hearing this incident, Shringi became very angry. He cursed King Parikshit by taking the water of the river in his hands, and chanting mantra said that this mischievous king will die due to the bite of Takshak Nag (deadly serpent) on the tenth day from today.

After some time, the meditation of Shamik Rishi was over and he saw that a snake was wrapped around his neck. Then he smiled softly and asked who has done this joke with him? Then the children of the ashram narrated everything to him. Then the Shamik Rishi meditated and came to know from his insights that the king was none other than the glorious, fair King Parikshit, who had done this misconduct due to the ill effects of the Kalyuga who was hiding in his crown at that time.

When Shamik Rishi came to know that his son Shringi had cursed King Parikshit due to extreme anger, he felt very sad. He reprimanded his son Shringi and said that for a small mistake, you have given a big punishment to a gentle, judicious and benevolent king, whose mind was polluted by Kalyuga. Shamik Rishi felt very sad about the behaviour of his son Shringi and said that misuse of power is very unrighteous.

King Parikshit returned to his palace from hunting and put off the golden crown from his head. As soon as he put off the golden crown, the influence of Kalyuga had gone from his mind. Then he remembered that he had committed a grave sin by wrapping the dead snake around the neck of Shamik Rishi. He thought that he would go to his ashram in the morning and apologize to him for his misconduct.

King Parikshit was very upset by this incident. Meanwhile, at night, the gatekeeper informed King Parikshit that Shamik Rishi wants to meet him. King Parikshit himself came to the palace gate and welcomed Shamik Rishi and took him inside the palace. He washed his feet with water and offered flowers on his feet and bowed down before him. Then the Shamik Rishi said that - Oh king! I came to know about the incident through meditation that you had done such an act due to the ill effects of the Kalyuga who was hiding in your golden crown at that time. Shamik Rishi further said that, Oh king! I am informing you with acute pain that my son Shringi has cursed you with a terrible curse, due to which you will live for only ten days. Hearing this, King Parikshit's wife fainted and there was sadness all around the palace. But King Parikshit was not disturbed on hearing this sad news and said whatever is destined, will happen. Perhaps this is the will of the God. King Parikshit apologised to Shamik Rishi for his indecent behaviour and told him that the punishment given by his son was justified. I must be punished for my sin. King Parikshit respectfully sent Shamik Rishi out of the palace and immediately called his Kul guru. King Parikshit asked the Kul guru that only ten days of his life are left, what should he do in this situation?

The Kul guru advised King Parikshit that now he should hand over the administration of the kingdom to his son Janamejaya and go towards the forest for the penance. The Kul guru told King Parikshit that before going to the forest, he should consult Mahatma Shukdev Ji for his blessings and guidance and he should spend the rest of his life time according to his advice.

According to the advice of Kul guru, King Parikshit handed over the reins of his kingdom to his son Janamejaya and went straight away to the ashram of Mahatma Shukdev ji and touched his feet and prayed for his blessings and guidance. Mahatma Shukdev Ji told King Parikshit that he had known all the events with his divine vision. Shukdev Ji said - Oh king! Do not waste your time even for few second. He said that considering this body to be mortal, become detached from this world and concentrate to meditation and devotion of God. This body is composed of five elements and will merge into the five elements. You engage your mind completely in God. By forgetting yourself and devoting to God through meditation and prayer you can get liberation.

The ten days of this story has symbolic meaning. Ten days of life means that this life is temporary and death is true. Nobody knows when and how death will come. Therefore, considering this life as uncertain and mortal, one should lead life in this world like a karmyogi without attachment and hatred and should take recourse to meditation and devotion to attain enlightenment or divine knowledge so that one can get rid of the cycle of birth and death.

21
IMPORTANCE OF GURU

'Guru' is a Sanskrit language word. This term is often used for a teacher or guide, but in ancient time the importance of the Guru was more than that of a teacher. In Sanskrit 'Guru' means who helps his disciple in removing darkness i.e., ignorance and leads the disciple to light i.e., knowledge. The Guru helps him to dispel the delusion from the mind by clarifying the difference between untruth and truth, Brahma and Maya. The Guru helps the disciple in moulding his values. The Guru helps in the spiritual development of the disciple through his experience and knowledge gained from the penance and deep meditation practice.

'Guśabdastvandhakāraḥ syāt ruśabdastannirodhakaḥ,
Andhakāranirodhitvād gururityabhidhīyate.'

The syllable 'gu' means darkness, the syllable 'ru' means he who dispels them,

Because of the power to dispel darkness, the guru is thus named.
(Advayataraka Upanishad, Verse –16)
Saint Tulsidas has prayed to his Guru in this way -

'Bandau guru pad kanj kripa sindhu nar roop hari
Mahamoh Tam Punj Jasu Bachan Ravi Kar Nikar.'

This means, a Guru is like God in the human form and an ocean of grace and compassion, whose words are like sun-rays which remove the thick cloud of attachment.

Saint Kabir has described the importance of Guru in the following words-

'Moh nadi bikral hai koi na utre par
Satguru Kebat Saath Lei, Hans Hoy Jam Nyar. '

Saint Kabir compares the attachment to this world like a horrible river and said that it is very difficult to cross this river without the help of a sailor, who sails the boat safely. He further says that a guru can help like a sailor to cross the horrible river of attachment. He further compares the maya or delusion with Yama. One can overcome on yama just as a duck who swims safely.

"Sumiran Marag Sahaj ka, Sadguru Diya Batai,
Sas sas sumiran karu yek din milsi aaye."

The path to remembrance of God is very simple. Sadhguru has told us this.

We should remember God in every breath. One day God will definitely meet us.

Saint Kabir further says –

'Timir Gaya Ravi dekhte kumati gai guru gyan
Sumati gai ati lobhte bhakti gai abhiman.'

The teachings of guru dispel the ignorance just as the darkness disappears when the sun appears. The end of delusion is possible with the knowledge of Guru. The wisdom vanishes due to the excessive greed and the devotion goes away due to arrogance.

There were tradition of Guru and disciple for a long period in ancient India. From the Vedic period, the disciples used to learn spiritual knowledge as well as martial arts and music from their gurus while sitting near the sages, maharishis and saints. There were many gurukuls where various types of education were given. While Parshuram and Dronacharya were great gurus of defence skills, Maharishi Kapil, sage Gautama were masters of theosophy and philosophy. Similarly, the names of Guru Atri, Yajnavalkya, Agastya, Vishwamitra, Sandipani, Panini, Maharishi Kanad, Maharishi Vasishta, Vardhman Mahaveer, Gautama Buddha, Sant Kabir, Guru Nanak, Guru Gorakhnath and Sant Ravidas can be mentioned as prominent gurus.

Guru Vashishta and Maharishi Vishwamitra were the gurus of Shri Rama. Shri Krishna had his education in the Gurukul of Maharishi Sandipani. King Janaka was educated by the famous Guru Rishi Yajnavalkya. Gautama Buddha received yoga lessons from Alara Kalama and Uddaka Ramaputta. Similarly, the Guru of Sant Kabir was Swami Ramanand. Saint Tulsi Das's Guru was Narharidas. Totapuri was guru of Rama Krishna Paramhansa. Meera Bai's guru was Sant Ravidas ji. The Guru of Swami Vivekananda was Ram Krishna Paramhansa. Guru of Shankaracharya was Govind Bhagavatpada.

Upanishad means to sit near the Guru and seek knowledge. There were very hard examinations for getting admission in Gurukul. The Guru used to test the mind of the student whether he is worthy of this knowledge or not. They were of the view that the wrong person would misuse the knowledge of spirituality and yoga and would harm mankind by exploiting others.

But nowadays, due to the commercialization of the entire system, the old meaning of Guru has completely changed. There was a time in ancient India when yoga and spirituality were considered a symbol of renunciation, penance, self-control, quietness and devotion. Yoga and spirituality enumerate the four natural sanctuaries namely: silence, solitude, peace and simplicity. But now everywhere there is a web of display, pretence, advertisement, hypocrisy and confusion which is distracting the minds of the people from the main objective of spirituality and yoga pushing them towards delusion, ignorance, lust and darkness. However, the aim of yoga and spirituality is to remove all kinds of flaws i.e., sexual desire, anger, greed, ego, attachment, envy and to connect oneself to God through purity of mind.

In the Aranyakand of Ramcharit Manas, in the dialogue between Shri Rama and Narada, Shri Rama narrates the qualities of saints to Narada Muni and says that-

'Sad Bikar Jit Anagh Akama, Achal Akinchan Suchi Sukhdhama.
Amit Bodh Anih Mitabhogi, Satyasar Kabi Kobind Jogi.'

That is, the saints are those who have conquered over all the six vices, namely, sexual desire, anger, greed, attachment, ego and jealousy. To be sinless, devoid of cravings, innocent, stable mind, prudence, equanimity, purity from within and outside, centre of happiness, knowledgeable, desireless, moderate eater, truthful, learned and yogi by nature are the qualities of the saints. But nowadays, fake spiritual and yoga gurus have started accumulating wealth by selling this sacred knowledge as a product by making it spicy. In fact, the so-called gurus have now become businessmen and are doing business worth billions of rupees which is contrary to the basic tenets of yoga and spirituality. This is a terrible tragedy of Kalyuga. The ancient meaning of Guru has completely changed. Just as a blind person is incapable of showing the way to another person, similarly a person who is full of various kinds of vices and lusts and is wandering in the darkness of ignorance, cannot be the Guru of another person.

Thus, those who are inclined to seek spiritual growth, peace, bliss and liberation from the bondage of birth and death, that is, aspiring for nirvana or moksha or salvation, must stay away from the fake gurus. The fake guru will push others on wrong path and eventually the life of the disciple would be spoiled. A real guru is one who keeps himself away from publicity. He leads a very simple life. He does not accumulate wealth. He has blotless character and is a depository of wisdom. There may be some real guru in Buddhism due to its strict laws. However, in other religion there is complete darkness. Therefore, seeing the darkness all around, one should go for spiritual journey without guru taking example of Lord Buddha who had achieved the highest knowledge by his own efforts. He got only elementary knowledge from his gurus.

Yoga and spirituality are not a profession, but a path to find oneself. If the right guru is found, then the path becomes a little easier. But nowadays it is rare to find the right guru. Lord Buddha and Lord Mahavira had left their kingdoms, lavish life and luxuries, and left their palaces in search of the truth. But nowadays the hypocritical saints and yoga gurus are earning money by selling this sacred knowledge. Looking at the era of this downfall today, one should start the spiritual journey by considering the idol of Lord Shiva, the supreme master of spirituality and yoga, as the supreme Guru. One should resort to the means like pranayama, meditation, solitude, silence, piety, peace and detachment of mind and senses from the world. Only through quietness, meditation and knowledge a person can achieve the ultimate goal of life in which the grace of God is indispensable. Nothing can be obtained without the grace of God. Saint Tulsi Das says that one can adopt multiple measures for years but the wisdom cannot be gained without the grace of lord shiva. Saint Kabir says that if all seven oceans are converted into ink and the whole world is used like a paper even then it would be impossible to write about the glory and virtues of God. In fact, God is the ultimate guru. It was because of the grace of God that foolish Kalidas became the great poet. Valmiki could become great Maharshi from a bandit. Thus, any person can become great by the grace of God and through the right karma.

22
IGNORANCE IS THE BONDAGE OF LIFE

The teachings of jnana yoga, devotion yoga and karma yoga were given by Shri Krishna to Arjuna in Bhagwat Gita. The teachings of Lord Buddha, the sermon of Saint Kabir, the Yoga Sutras of Maharishi Patanjali and the teachings of the Upanishads have advised the human being that this samsara is changeable, mortal and everything is impermanent in this world. Therefore attachment with anything in this world is ignorance. Human mind and senses make the people attached to this world. Sexual desires, anger, greed, fear, ego and jealousy are created due to ignorance which are the cause of unhappiness. Attachment happens in both love and hate. In either situations of like or dislike the mind remains obsessed with subjects. Lord Buddha said 'Sarvam Dukham' (There is suffering) and Guru Nanak said that 'Dukhiya sab Sansar,' i.e., people everywhere in this world are unhappy. The cause of unhappiness in this world is attachment to things or persons. Both like and dislike are born out of ignorance, that is, when human beings do not understand the eternal truth of nature that everything in this world is temporary and perishable, then the feeling of attachment or hate arise. That is why Saint Kabir says – 'Kabira khada bazar me sabke mangat khair, Na kahu se dosti Na kahu se bair'. It means Kabir is wishing for the wellbeing of everyone while standing in the market (world), he has neither attachment nor enmity to anyone.

Lord Buddha, while giving his last sermon to the Buddhist monks before Mahaparinirvana said that you must come out of the delusion and become awakened. 'Aapo dipo bhava', lit up the lamp of wisdom inside through meditation. Forget what I have said to you, rather you should search the truth by your own efforts. Don't waste your time. Withdraw your mind and senses from this world and become introvert and go inside. Then only you will be able to discover the truth. It is mandatory to follow modesty before meditation. Good character is the condition precedent for the meditation. Thereafter, you can get intuitive power through meditation and gradually the darkness of ignorance will be removed and you can attain enlightenment.

In the Bhagavad Gita, Lord Krishna advised Arjuna and said -

Oh Partha! You should develop equanimity and remain in the wisdom and do your duty without attachment. Then Arjuna asked Lord Shri Krishna about the nature of a person having serene mind. Then Shri Krishna told Arjuna that the person whose mind remains calm and stable in every situation, whose worldly craving have ended and there is no turmoil in the mind and he remains completely unaffected in the situation of pleasure and pain, love and hate and who becomes fearless, such a person can be said to have stable intellect. (Bhagavad Gita - 2/56).

The entire Upanishads say, 'Brahma Satya, Jagat Mithya', which means that Brahma (God) is the only truth, that is, all creatures, nature are creations of God, but due to delusion the feeling of difference arises. The Chhandogya Upanishad states, 'Tat tvam Asi' (tattvamsi) which means that Brahman is in you, me and everyone. Sage Aruni Uddālaka explains to his son Shvetaketu that as the different types of jewelleries made of gold have different forms and names but their basic element is gold, similarly all beings are made of the consciousness. Only the names and forms of all beings are different which leads us to the feeling of duality, but basically, we all are divine. This is what Krishna says in the Bhagavad Gita - 'Sarvasya chahna hridi sannivishto', that is, I live in the heart of all beings. (Bhagavad Gita - 15/15).

Saint Kabir says that,

"Kasturi kundal base, mrig dhoondhe ban maahi,
Aise ghat ghat Ram hain, duniya dekhe nahi."

The musk is in the umbilicus but the deer searches for it in the forest. In the same way, God is present inside everybody but people don't realise him.

Saint Kabir further observes in another couplet in Hindi- 'Moko kahan durhe Re Bande, Main to tere Pas Re.'

"Where do you search me, dear?
I'm near you
Neither I am in a shrine nor in an idol
Neither I am in temple nor in mosque
Neither I am at Kaaba nor at Kilash
I am close to you
I am near you."

Actually, man himself does not know about his true nature. It is true that the human body is made up of five senses of perception, five karma senses, Mind, seven Dhatu, five Kosha, five elements, but in reality, this body is lifeless without the consciousness which is experienced in the state of samadhi. In fact, the human mind is so much engaged in the family, social, communal, political matters that one cannot find mental space to think over about one's own true nature. The human senses always keep wandering in the world and in the subjects of desire, due to which man does not realize himself. Self-realization happens only when he becomes detached from the world and discovers himself through meditation. In the state of samadhi he becomes aware of his true nature.

In the spiritual journey, meditation plays an important role. Since ancient times, sages and monks used to meditate in seclusion in the caves and forests. They tried to understand the theosophy and the cosmic mysteries. The idols of Lord Shiva are depicted in yoga posture. Lord Buddha, Lord Mahavira and many Mahatmas and Maharishis have discovered the ultimate truth through meditation.

Today, human beings have fallen into the well of ignorance. Jealousy due to selfishness and greed to accumulate excessive wealth is increasing. Due to this, many kinds of mental evils have arisen in the mind of human beings which will ultimately affect the karma. People are not aware of the outcome of bad karma which would eventually lead them to wander in many realms. The saints and Mahatmas have repeatedly said that human life is the best, every human being should understand it. It is said that there are millions creatures in this universe. Human life is superior among all these creatures. Human beings have high ability of understanding. His consciousness is more developed than other creatures. The animals spend their lives only in food, sex and sleep. If a human being too dies after spending his life only in food, sex and sleep, then it would be like animal life. If a man does not understand the value of this life and is ignorant about the ultimate goal, that is, freedom from the cycle of birth and death, then his human life is meaningless. Saint Tulsi Das said – 'Bade Bhagya manush tan pawa sur durlabh sadagranthin gawa.' That is, a human life is achieved by great fortune. It is in this human life that a person can attain salvation by attaining enlightenment or Brahma Gyan. The entire universe is a manifestation of God, but people cannot understand it due to the ignorance.

Due to human ignorance, caste, Varna system, superstition, hypocrisy, rituals and communal evils are in vogue. People do not come out of ignorance till the time of death.

Having seen all this, Saint Kabir says –

'Kabira kahe yah jag andha, andhi jaisi gay, bachhda tha so mar gaya, jhuti cham chatay.'Saint Kabir says that, as a cow who behaves like a blind due to the attachment to her calf who has already died and even then, a cow goes on licking the dead calf. Similarly, the human beings behave like blind person due to ignorance.

Saint Kabir again refers to the ignorance of sectarian people and says,

'Na Jane tera sahib kaisa hai?
Masjid bhitar mulla pukare, kya sahib tera bahra hai?

Chiuti ke pag newar baje, so bhi sahib sunta hai.
Pandit hoke asan mare lambi mala japta hai,
Andar tere kapat kartani so bhi sahib lakhta hai.'

'Don't you know how your master is?
Mulla is calling loudly inside the mosque, is your master deaf?
The lord even hears the footsteps of small ants,
The priest is just shuffling the rosery beads in sitting posture,
The lord is watching your deceit.'

Saint Kabir considers attachment to the family as a big ignorance –

'Pata tuta dal se le gai pawan udai, Abke bichhde kab milege dur padege jay.'

When the leaves of the tree are blown away by the wind and they became invisible, then the tree says that it does not know when they will meet again?

Pointing out about the impermanence and changeability of this world and human life, Saint Kabir says that this family union is also temporary. After death, who knows who will reborn in which of the realms. Everyone's future will vary according to their karma.

Today there is darkness of ignorance all around. The man is walking in unconsciousness state. He is not caring about moral values by resorting to lies and deception. He is unaware of the consequences of his actions. He does not know what has been said in the scriptures. The story of Nachiketa in 'Katho Upanishad' is on this subject.

The story of Nachiketa is described in the Katho Upanishad. Nachiketa's father Bajashrava was a sage. He performed the Vishvajit Yagna. In this yagna, the organizer had to donate all his property. The boy Nachiketa was deeply disappointed when he saw that his father was only donating old, weak and sick cows instead of healthy cows which could not give milk. Seeing this, Nachiketa thought that his father would not get good result from this yagna. He should try to wake up his father from attachment to wealth. To bring out father from the attachment, Nachiketa asked his father, to whom are you donating me? Rishi Bajashrava ignored this question. But Nachiketa again asked this question to his father. On repeatedly asking the same question, Rishi Bajashrava became enraged and told Nachiketa that – I am donating you to Yamraj (the God of death). Nachiketa was saddened by his father's words but to keep his father words and for his benefit, Nachiketa reached Yamloka.

On reaching the door of Yamraj, Nachiketa came to know that Yamraj was not there. He had gone elsewhere. Hearing this news, Nachiketa was not disappointed and sat at the door of Yamraj waiting for him for three days without eating and drinking. After returning from outside, Yamraj came to know about Nachiketa from the gatekeeper that the child has come here to save his father's words. Yamraj became very happy to see Nachiketa's allegiance to his father. Yamraj said to Nachiketa - Rishi Kumar, you have been waiting for me at my door for three days without taking food and water. But your time has not yet come for Yamloka. Therefore, you should return to your home by taking any three boons from me. Then Nachiketa asked Yamraj for the first boon that upon returning home, his father's affection for him should remain same as before. Then Yamaraj said – all right, I grant you this boon to you. Then Nachiketa expressed his desire to know about the brahma and the soul from Yamraj in the second boon and in the third boon Nachiketa wanted to know about effect after the death from Yamraj. Then Yamraj said to Nachiketa that you are a child right now and instead of knowing about the deep and subtle matters related to theosophy and soul you should ask boon for worldly pleasures and grandeur which is generally aspired by worldly people. Then Nachikata told Yamraj that -

Oh, revered Yamraj! You know it very well that the sensual pleasures are transitory and human beings can never be satisfied with money. Just like adding ghee to a fire, the fire is stirred, in the same way, the attainment of wealth and material enjoyment increases the desire for material enjoyment. Where there is craving, how can there be peace or satisfaction? In this way, man will always be burning in the fire of imperfection and dearth. No wise person can ask for such painful wealth and enjoyment. I will only need a little money for living, which will be obtained by your grace. This life is fleeting, so I am desirous to know about the liberation from this life cycle by enlightening myself through the subject of theology and the soul. (27, 1st Valli, Katho Upanishad).

While teaching Nachiketa about theosophy, Yamraj said, when a blind person is showing the way to another blind person, then such a person will not reach to his destination rather he would wander in the middle of the path or suffer from variety of pains by hitting to the stones, colliding to animals or walls or falling into the ditches or facing more similar difficulties or misery. Similarly, if a man has no realisation or knowledge of theosophy or soul, he will suffer a lot from life to life by taking birth in various creatures like animal, insects and so on or by entering into the hell he would suffer for eternity. Those who consider themselves to be intelligent and have disregard for sacred scriptures or ignore the theology and knowledge of soul and consider worldly and sensual pleasures as their goal, such human beings waste their lives in ignorance. (5, Second Valli, Katho Upanishad).

Yamraj further says to Nachiketa that - Oh Nachiketa! A man who does not understand the importance of his life and is fascinated by money for the attainment of worldly pleasures and has craving for luxury and indulges in sensual pleasures and has obsessed mind, is an ignorant man. There is a lack of purity and awakening in the mind of such human beings and such people are bound to bear the fruits of their karmas and take birth again and again in various forms due to their karmas. Such ignorant people do not believe in rebirth and do not think about liberation from this life cycle. (6, Second Valli, Katho Upanishad).

In addition to Hindu, Jain or Buddhist literatures, in the fourth chapter of Maharishi Patanjali's Yoga Sutra the means of attaining liberation from the infinite cycle of birth and death, that is, salvation, has been described. The Kaivalya or Nirvana or Moksha can be attained not after death, but in this life itself. The meaning of Moksha, Kaivalya or Nirvana is the same. Different religions have used different names. This is a state of sadhana where all worldly attachment and craving of the seeker are eliminated. The mind becomes clean, that is, without faults or the illness such as lecherous desire, anger, greed, attachment, ego, fear and malice. Avidya is completely removed and knowledge (jnana) is attained and all delusions and worries are dispelled. After reaching such a state, life becomes illuminated. Such person remains in equanimity amidst both happiness and sorrow. Such a person loves all living beings and remain blissful. Such people are called enlightened.

Maharishi Patanjali has described the means like, Yama, Niyama, Pranayama (breathing exercise), Pratyahara i.e., detachment of mind and senses from worldly subjects and regular meditation to reach the stage of Kaivalya in his yoga sutra. Whereas in Buddhist literature ten virtues have been enumerated to reach to the stage of Nirvana which are also called paramitas. It is imperative to develop paramita such as generosity, modesty (good conduct), renunciation, intuition, enthusiasm, patience, truthfulness, determination to achieve the goal, compassion and mental equanimity etc. However, the Buddhist literatures have also dealt with the ten obstructions in the way of nirvana namely, lustful desire, anger, conceit, negative thoughts, wrong rituals, superstitions, attachment to bad habits, longing for intoxication, jealousy, mental anxiety and ignorance. Vipassana meditation has great importance in Buddhism. The regular practice of vipassana will control the volatile mind and capricious senses and lead to equanimity.

In the Bhagavad Gita, Lord Shri Krishna said to Arjuna that the senses do not disturb a wise person amidst adverse situations like pain and pleasure. Such person has stable mind. He is disinterested in worldly lusts and attachment and is qualified for salvation. (Bhagavad Gita - 2/15).

23
CAUSES OF HUMAN SUFFERING

In this world, there is unrest, hatred and anxiety in place of peace, love and bliss and this is the reason that there is bitterness all around. There are quarrels, crime, terror, fear, restlessness, corruption and discontent in the world. Actually, man's inner nature wants peace and happiness, but due to ignorance the human's life is filled with unrest and sorrow. Unhappiness is a mental and emotional state. If the mind is made clean by removing the negativity of the mind, then a man can get wisdom, thereafter there will be an end of suffering from his life.

Two great men who were born long ago on this earth had suggested the remedy for human suffering. Lord Buddha discovered the cause of man's suffering through meditation and then he found the solution. Later on, Maharishi Patanjali also found a way for the end of the human suffering.

Maharishi Patanjali said that as long as a human being remains under the influence of 'five obstacles,' or pancha klesha he will not get relief from sorrows, because Panch kleshas are the main cause of unhappiness. In the second chapter of Yoga Sutras, from sutras three to nine, Maharishi Patanjali has described five obstacles namely, Avidya (ignorance), Asmita (ego), Raga (attachment), Dwesha (hatred) and Abhinivesh (fear). Maharishi Patanjali says that it is because of these five obstacles that man suffers from sorrow.

According to Maharishi Patanjali, the root cause of human suffering is ignorance because all kleshas (obstacles) originate from it. Suffering may be due to physical illness or dearth of money but the main reason for man's grief is mental and emotional which is generated due to spiritual ignorance. Ignorance of spirituality means the unawareness of own self. After all, what is human being? Is human being just a structure of bones and flesh or the body made of the five elements or just a combination of the microscopic molecules? A man cannot be alive without consciousness inside the structure of that body. A dead human body is called a corpse which is burnt or buried in the ground. Thus, man's real existence is due to the consciousness and not knowing about the consciousness is spiritual ignorance. Therefore, to know about consciousness is to know about own self.

Human beings are committing big mistake by not knowing their own true nature and forgetting about the consciousness. This is due to the hunger for sensual pleasures. They have accumulated sufferings due to sensual pleasures. They have become prey to many kinds of wrong notions and habits due to the sensual pleasure. Many types of drug addiction, lust and inappropriate expectations from family members have added emotional grief to human's life.

Though there is possibility of infinite bliss within human beings which can be attained by meditation and pranayama, but most human beings are unaware of it. They consider sensual joy to be pleasure, whereas sensory pleasure is ephemeral, because the senses cannot be satisfied with one kind of pleasure, but rather they seek different types of pleasures in new objects and in the end, there is desperation.

Happiness is an inside matter. Only delusion is outside. The person who has attained that bliss of the divine within, will not be interested in the external pleasure of the senses. Saint Surdas says that when a bee has tasted the juice of lotus flower then why it will taste a bitter flower? Meera says that the treasure of happiness derived from devotion to the Lord is such that even a thief cannot steal it and it will keep on increasing day by day. Those are blessed people who have tasted the ecstasy of God through meditation in the state of samadhi. They will not be inclined for sensual pleasure.

Lord Buddha used to say that man is often not guided by his conscience but by the emotions of the mind. Emotions are the product of ignorance which do not have the ability to analyse any fact and emotions create sorrow. Lord Buddha further said that the mind is the vanguard of all tendencies. If a person acts with a corrupt mind, grief follows him as the wheel of a bullock cart follows the hooves of oxen and if a man does something with a pure mind, then happiness follows him in the same way as his shadow moves with him. Lord Buddha laid great emphasis on meditation and wisdom. Meditation keeps the mind calm and produces wisdom. Buddha used to say that man creates misery on his own due to the ignorance. A man creates his own sorrow through imprudent tendencies like craving, hatred, greed and attachment. Lord Buddha used to say that one should just witness the feelings arising in his mind through Vipassana meditation so that the corrupt thoughts do not enter into mind, because the corrupt thought causes misery as well as spoils the good karma.

The idea of Lord Buddha was very precise and clear like the rules of modern psychology. According to psychology, positive thinking makes the thinking pattern of the mind positive and creates the same type of conditioning of the mind. Similarly negative thinking makes the thinking pattern of the mind negative, that is, the mind thinks in the same patten and ultimately it becomes a habit.

Twenty-five hundred years ago, whatever was said by Lord Buddha about the mind, the same thing was said by modern-day Russian physiologist Ivan Pavlov, who received the Nobel Prize in 1904 on the principle of conditioning of the mind.

Lord Buddha discovered very subtle knowledge in his entire life by experimenting on himself like a researcher. He never gave any example of any scripture or book, nor did he give an example of others, but he learnt it through his own experiment. Lord Buddha often used to say that before accepting any opinion or idea, you should examine its veracity through your own experience and observation and then one should accept it. Lord Buddha used to say that one should give up the subjects that cause sorrow. Enjoyment will come on its own, because pleasure is inherent in human nature. Keep on meditating, joy will come automatically.

Due to ignorance, various types of superstitions and misconception are spread among the people in the name of religion. Most of the people take bath in Ganges to wash sins in order to get salvation but Lord Buddha used to say that if there would be salvation by bathing in the Ganges, then frogs, crabs, fishes, tortoises, dolphins and crocodiles who live in the Ganges could have got salvation, but it does not happen. Salvation is attained only by the end of ignorance. Even today man is a victim of useless rituals, hypocrisy, superstitions and evils. There can be no good for a man through rituals.

Once upon a time, Lord Buddha was passing through a village. A ritualistic Brahmin was very angry with Lord Buddha, because Lord Buddha criticized the rituals as ignorance. He used to say that a man can improve his present as well as next life through his good karma and the ritual is just ignorance. Due to this, the business of ritualistic Brahmins came to a standstill. The ritualistic Brahmin abused Lord Buddha after seeing him. Then Lord Buddha said, 'Is your talk complete, should I leave now?' Then the ritualistic Brahmin said – 'I have been abusing you.' Then Lord Buddha said that 'this would have been a matter of abuse for me years back when I was not awakened, but now I will not punish myself for the mistake of others. If you are abusing then all right, you know about your job, I will not accept your abuse.' Lord Buddha went forward calmly and happily, but that ritualistic Brahmin became very disturbed and he kept on thinking all night that he had abused the great seer and has committed the sin. Next day the ritualistic Brahmin went to apologize to the Lord Buddha. Lord Buddha was staying near another village. That ritualistic Brahmin said, – 'Forgive me, Oh Buddha!' Lord Buddha said, 'I did not accept your words. The matter was over, but you are still carrying the same things in your mind. Get those things out of your mind and keep calm.'

According to Maharishi Patanjali, the second cause of suffering is asmita i.e., arrogance (ego). There is a very precise line in a poem that states, ' When the time of downfall of man comes, the wisdom dies first. The ego has been considered a major flaw in the scriptures. Man's conscience is destroyed due to ego. Due to ego, man harms himself and he also harms others. The whole of Lanka burned to ashes due to Ravana's arrogance. Due to Kansh's ego, he and his people were destroyed. Duryodhana's arrogance led to the battle of Mahabharata. Lord Shri Krishna had asked Duryodhana for only five villages for the Pandavas, but Duryodhana told Lord Shri Krishna that he would not give them land even equal to the tip of a needle due to arrogance. This incident was the immediate cause of the battle of Mahabharata and as a result, all the Kauravas were destroyed. Hitler and Mussolini's arrogance led to the Second World War and millions of people from Europe and many other countries were killed and trillions of properties were destroyed.

At the time of the battle of Mahabharata, Mahatma Vidur asked Lord Krishna – 'Oh Lord! You had asked for only five villages for the five Pandavas, but Duryodhana turned down your proposal. Why did Duryodhana behave like this with his cousins?' Then Lord Krishna told Mahatma Vidura that Duryodhana's mind was filled with ego due to which his conscience had died. Lord Shri Krishna further said that due to excessive tamo guna and rajo guna i.e., craving and hatred, the demonic tendency is born. In Bhagavad Gita Shri Krishna says to Arjuna, 'Oh Partha! Arrogance, pride, anger, callousness and ignorance - all these are the symptoms of devilish instincts.' (Bhagavad Gita - 16/4).

Buddhist organisation established by Lord Buddha were joined by many kings, princes, sons of big merchants and their relatives. Lord Buddha himself was the son of a Maharaja. Ananda was also his cousin. All the members of the Sangh had to forget their family background and take the bowl for alms. Taking the begging bowl meant removing one's own ego of wealth, position and high family pride. As long as the ego persists, the path of spiritual journey cannot be followed and nirvana will not be achieved. Ego is considered the biggest barrier for the attainment of nirvana.

In Sikhism too, the gurus had laid the foundation of such traditions through which the arrogance of the rich and the high in society could be erased. Through hand service (kar seva), the rich and high-ranking people also have to clean the shoes and slippers of the common people and women of rich families also have to bake breads and cook for others in the Gurudwaras. This tradition is followed to remove the ego and to increase their faith in Waheguru. Guru Nanak often used to say that every human being is the creation of the same Waheguru and hating anyone is like hating the creation of God.

Maharishi Patanjali considers attachment and hatred respectively as the third and fourth cause of human suffering. In fact, Attachment and hatred are two sides of the same coin. In both cases, the mind becomes attached and destroys the wisdom. Therefore, both attachment and hatred should be avoided. The Gopis of Vrindavan became enamoured with Shri Krishna. Sant Surdas ji says -

'Jit Dekho Tit Shyam Mayi Hai, Shyam Kunj Ban Madhuvan Shyama Shyam Gagan Ghan Ghata Chhai Hai', that is, the Gopis had become mad in love of shri Krishna. That is why Shri Krishna sent Uddhav to convince the Gopis that they should forgot him and must worship God. Then the Gopis conveyed to Uddhav –'Ye Uddhav, man Na bhaye das bis, ek huto so gayo shyam sang, ko aradhe ish.' Means, the mind is not ten or twenty, only one mind which we had, has gone with shri Krishna, now who will worship God? Ultimately Uddhava failed to convince the Gopis. Similar was the condition of Kansa. He used to hate Shri Krishna so much that he could see Krishna everywhere and Kansa's condition had become like an insane. Therefore, both attachment and aversion destroy wisdom. Love and hate are created by the mind. In both love and hate the mind becomes attached to an object, subject or person, i.e., in both situations, the mind does not have the capacity for independent thinking. Thus, man becomes biased, i.e., the sense of fairness and objectivity ceases. In both attachment and malice, wisdom is lost due to the growth of tamoguna and rajoguna.

To understand attachment and hatred it is important to understand the nature of the mind. When a person develops affection for his family members, pet dog, domesticated cattle, house or car, the attachment occupies his mind. This attachment leads to grief in adverse conditions. In case of the death of a pet animal, sorrow is caused to the person due to emotional attachment with the pet and in some cases, it creates unbearable suffering. Similarly, many people become jealous and disturbed due to particular person, object or subject. The mind becomes unhappy due to hatred or malice. This is why Lord Buddha used to say that the mind should be liberated from the negativity, that is, detachment of mind from attachment and hatred and to stay in equanimity. Maharishi Patanjali's 'pratyahara' means withdrawal of the mind and senses from external subjects.

In the Bhagavad Gita, Lord Shri Krishna says that those who subdue their mind and senses, whose mind is made introvert, who keeps the mind and senses detached from external subjects through meditation and devotion to God, they get happiness as an outcome and such persons become free from attachment and hatred. (Bhagavad Gita - 2/64).

Lord Buddha used to say that the greatest conqueror in this world is not the one who has defeated hundreds of his enemies by winning hundreds of battles, but the great warrior is the one who has conquered his mind and senses. Lord Vardhman, the last Tirthankara of Jainism, is called Mahavira because he had conquered his mind and senses. The word 'Jitendra' derived from the word 'Jin', means the person who has conquered his senses. Whoever has conquered his mind and senses, his suffering ceases to exist.

Maharishi Patanjali in his yoga sutra considers the fifth cause of grief as abhinivesh i.e., fear. Man is always afraid due to some or other reason. The fear of loss of wealth, honour, position, fear of disease or death, fear of illness or death of any member of the family makes the man unhappy. In the 31st verse of the book 'Vairagya Satak', King Bharthari says that the fear of disease on consuming more delicious food, the fear of slander if born in a high family, the fear of robbery on possessing more wealth, the fear of enemies when one is strong, fear of demon on silence, fear of debate on the scriptures, fear of evildoers when one is gentle, fear of Yamraj on having a good body, that is, everything in this world is a cause for fear. Only person with detachment or vairagya can be free from fear.

Man remains attached to his body and remains fearful and unhappy due to old age, sickness or death. But the fear cannot distract a person who has wisdom. Socrates was very calm when he was wrongly made accused of corrupting the youth by his thoughts, speeches and when the jury of the orthodox government awarded death sentence to him, then a disciple of Socrates asked him, 'are you not at all distracted by the death sentence while many people are crying after hearing this sentence?' Socrates said that 'I am feeling liberated from the bondage of this mortal body and I am feeling blissful.' When some well-wishers of Socrates advised him to flee from the jail, he turned down their advice and said that the attachment to this mortal body is ignorance. Socrates happily gave up his life after drinking a cup of poison.

In the Bhagavad Gita, Shri Krishna explains to Arjuna that - 'Oh Partha! There will be end of this body, but the soul is imperishable. This soul cannot be cut by any weapon, the fire cannot burn it, the water cannot wet it and the air cannot dry it. Therefore, you should give up the fear of death.' (Bhagavad Gita - 2/23).

24
HOW TO PURIFY THE MIND?

When Bhagirathi (Ganga) emerges from Gomukh in Uttarkashi, the water of the Ganges is perfectly clean, but when the Ganges passes through the plains of Uttar Pradesh and Bihar and meets the ocean in the Bay of Bengal, its water becomes dirty and is not fit for drinking. In the same way, the mind of a child of one or two years remains free from pollution or negativity, but gradually his mind gets polluted by social, communal, political and other kinds of negative environment. Therefore, when the mind is free from external negative environment or pollution, then it remains in its natural state, that is, it remains pure.

Both the eyes and the ears are the main conductors of pollution. They play the role of villain by taking pollution from outside and causing disorder in the mind. Therefore, it is very important to keep an eye on the activities of these two villains. A corrupt mind is the creator of all sins and unrighteousness. All the crimes committed by human beings in the world are the product of negative mind. The root cause of all kinds of sin and crime is the impurity of the mind. When the mind is pure, then it produces divine feelings, such as spiritual joy, friendliness, compassion, benevolence, non-violence and gratitude. But nowadays many people are worse than animals in human form. They are living in an unconscious state. They do not have good human qualities. It has been said in the religious texts that – 'Yesham na vidya, na tapo, na danam, gyanam na sheelam, na gunoh na dharmah, te mrityuloke bhuvi bharbhuta, manushyarupen mrigshcharanti.' That is, people without divine vidya, penance, charity, knowledge of scriptures, good conduct, virtues and dharma, are just like animal in this mortal world.

The root of all defilements inside a man is his polluted mind. The mind is the creator of negativity. The mind itself produces sexuality, anger, greed, ego, attachment and jealousy. In Buddhism the corrupt mind is referred as 'Mara', in Judaism, Christianity and Islam the corrupt mind is referred to as 'Satan' or 'Lucifer'. The devil or Lucifer mind always leads man to downfall by denying the divine sentiment. French philosopher René Descartes used to say that one should doubt on his mind and senses because they may mislead you, but you should rely on the intuition coming from the soul. For this reason, knowledgeable persons understand the activities of the mind and they are constantly engaged in the effort to purify the mind by doing yoga, meditation and service to the God.

Cleanliness of mind has great importance in spiritual life. The polluted mind is not suitable for yoga and spiritual practice. For this reason, before starting meditation it is necessary to follow Yama and Niyama as prescribed by Maharishi Patanjali in Yoga Sutra. Yama-niyama are the codes of ethics. In the same way, there is a lot of emphasis on the good conduct, ethics and good behaviour in the eight-fold path of Lord Buddha. After following the ethics, the meditation becomes easy. Therefore, purity of the mind is an essential element for spirituality and meditation.

Saint Kabir says categorically –

'Sab bhumi Varanasi, Sab neer ganga toye,
Gyani Aatam ram hai, Jo ghat nirmal hoye.'

That is, for those whose mind is pure, all the places are like the holy land of Varanasi and for those whose mind is pure, all the water is as holy as the Ganges water. Lord Rama resides in hearts of those whose mind is pure. If the mind is not clean then Rama cannot live there. If the mind is not clean then there is no benefit of undertaking pilgrimage or taking a bath in the Ganges.

Saint Kabir further says –

'Kabira man nirmal bhaya jaise ganga teer
Pichhe laga hari phire kahat Das Kabir.'

Saint Kabir says that, if the mind is pure, then God himself will search you. You need not search God, because God resides only in purity.

Highlighting the purity of the mind, 'the Bhagavata Purana' states that-"Shokamarshadibhirbhavirakrantam yasya manasam kantha tantra mukundasya utsambhavna bhavet" which means one whose mind is filled with anxiety, attachment, anger, greed and ego, in such mind how can Lord Mukunda (Shri Krishna) reside?

In the Ram Charit Manas, Shri Ram says -

'Nirmal man Jan so mohi paava, mohi kapat, chhal, chhidra Na bhava.' That is, a person having pure mind can only get me. I do not like hypocrites, deceptive and doubtful persons.

In the Bhagavad Gita, Lord Shri Krishna says to Arjuna –

'Ananyachetāḥ satatam yo māṁ smarati nityaśhaḥ
Tasyāhaṁ sulabhaḥ pārtha nitya-yuktasya yoginaḥ.'

'Oh Arjuna! Whosoever always and constantly think of me with undivided mind, to that Yogi ever absorbed in me, I am always attainable.' (Bhagavad Gita - 8/14).

If the mind becomes pure then there will be peace in the mind and where there is peace, there is happiness. Lord Buddha used to say that if the mind is pure, then joy fallows like the shadow. Buddha used to say, do not look at the faults of others, rather keep an eye on your own conducts and try to win peace over anger, good over evil, truth over untruth and benevolence over stinginess. But majority of the people do not understand the importance of purity of mind and they pollute the mind by putting various types of negative thoughts in the mind. Due to this their mind remains restless and such people are not able to differentiate between right and wrong. By thinking about dirty subjects regularly, the mind becomes conditional, as the mind of an alcoholic, smokers or blue film watcher keeps running after those objects again and again. In the Bhagavad Gita, Shri Krishna is saying-

'Uddharedātmanātmānaṃ nātmānamavasādayet
Ātmaiva hyātmano bandhurātmaiva ripurātmanaḥ.'

Elevate yourself through the power of your mind, and not degrade yourself, the mind can be the friend and also the enemy of the self. We are responsible for our own elevation or degradation. (Bhagwat Gita – 6/5)

In Brahmabindu Upanishad Verse - 2, it is said that-

'Mana eva manuṣyāṇāṃ kāraṇaṃ bandhamokṣayoḥ,
Bandhāya viṣayāsaktaṃ muktyai nirviṣayaṃ smṛtam.'

That is, the mind is the main cause for the bondage and liberation of human beings. Attachment of mind to the worldly sensory subjects are the causes of bondage and detachment of mind from the worldly craving is the cause of liberation, Moksha.

To understand the mind, it is important to understand the difference between the mind and the brain. The brain is a body part adjacent to the spinal cord in the anterior part of the head. It can be seen or touched, while the mind or Chita cannot be seen or touched. The brain performs the task of thinking, understanding, receiving information from all the senses through the nervous system and giving them directions. The brain is the centre of man's intelligence and distinguishes, analyses between right and wrong, while the mind or Chita is a type of wave generated by trillions of neurons inside the brain. This wave is called the flow of mind or Chita. For example, due to tide in the sea the waves continue to rise. These waves have no independent existence, but the water of ocean has its existence. Whatever a man watches through his eyes or hear through ears, the mind makes its own sense or perception of good or bad. This mind generates emotions and sometime makes us cry and laugh. The game of the mind, that is, its tide is always moving even in sleeping state through dreams, just like the tide of the sea. The sea wave is the same, but there are many types of waves in the mind. This is what Saint Kabir says –

'Sat samudra ki ek lahar, Mann ki lahar anek
Koi ek harijan ubara, doobi naw anek.'

That is, the waves of the seven oceans are the same, but the waves of different kinds of emotions keep emerging in the mind. Due to the waves of the mind, the life boats of many people sank except of some devotees of God, who do not come under the grip of these waves.

Maharishi Patanjali in his yoga sutra explains the remedy for controlling these waves of mind. To get rid of these waves of mind, Yama, Niyama, Asana, Pranayama, Pratyahara, Dharna (concentration on a point), meditation and Samadhi are mentioned. Lord Buddha's Vipassana meditation has been prescribed as the remedy to control the waves of mind. Buddha said that observe the rising emotions in your mind as a witness and see that what kind of waves are rising in the mind and for what reason.

Be aware of these different kinds of mood waves, Saint Kabir says –

'Mann ke mate na chaliye, Mann ke mate anek
Jo Mann par aswar hai, so sadhu koi ek.'

That is, do not go according to the rising emotions of the mind, rather go by the prudence. Those who keep their mind calm and stable through yoga and meditation, they are one in thousands.

In Bhagavad Gita, Lord Krishna is teaching Yoga to Arjuna and says that, oh son of Kunti! You should meditate by withdrawing your mind and senses from external subjects. Then Arjuna says that Oh Lord! This mind is very fickle, strong and rigid. Taming of mind is as difficult as stopping the current of air. Then Lord Shri Krishna is explaining to Arjuna that this mind is definitely difficult to be subdued but oh son of Kunti! this mind can be subdued by constant practice of detachment and meditation. (Bhagavad Gita - 6/35). Lord Krishna again says to Arjuna that yoga is impossible for those whose mind is not tamed. (Bhagavad Gita-6/36).

Saint Kabir tells about the nature of the mind -

'Yeh Mann maila neech hai, neech karam suhai
Amrit chharai Mann karai, vishai priti so khaye.'

This mind is dirty and lowly and it likes only low actions.

Knowingly leaves the nectar and takes only the sensual pleasures.

To make the mind clean, it is most important to keep the mind engaged in good work. Do not let the mind be fickle or sit completely idle, otherwise it will start running here and there like a fickle monkey. Apart from the domestic and other works, keep the mind engaged in morning and evening meditation and devotion to God. Silence, solitude, quietness and meditation are very important for spiritual and yoga practitioners.

Following remedies are given here to subdue the mind and purify it.

1. Make the mind detached from the world - Maharishi Patanjali says in the Yoga Sutra (1/15) that this world is witnessed only by the mind and the five senses. The eye sees, the ear hears, the nose smells, the skin touches and the tongue tastes and the mind makes its perception. The events seen and heard by the senses affect the mind. So do not watch or listen to bad events, because it has a very bad effect on the mind. Withdrawing the mind and the senses from the outside and making them introvert is Vairagya. The mind and the senses

are extrovert, they should be moulded to be introvert by detachment and meditation. Actually, the soul is the owner of this chariot (body) and the mind is the driver. The five sense organs of the body i.e., eyes, ears, nose, mouth and skin are the five horses of the chariot. If the soul is awakened then the person's life will go in the right direction, but if the owner of the chariot, that is, the soul, is in a dormant or sleeping state, the driver (mind) and five horses (five senses) will take the chariot on the wrong path. Therefore, it is absolutely necessary to wake up the soul by following meditation and modesty, otherwise the life will go in vain. The mind should be made to understand that this world is just an illusion, where everything is temporary. In fact, the world exists in the mind as you see it. Moreover, whatever you see with the eyes cannot be right. For example, when you look at an empty glass, it looks empty, but in reality, it is filled with air.

It is necessary for the detachment (vairagya) to know about oneself. That this body is perishable, only consciousness (soul) is eternal. The body dies but the soul is immortal. The soul is called the charioteer of this body. When the soul leaves this body, it becomes dead, this body becomes without charioteer. Then people take the dead body to the crematorium or burial ground and slowly people forget everything. The world goes on as usual. This is why this world has been called a fair. The fair is a temporary venue. The permanent ties should be made only with God who has sent the soul in a particular body.

2. Make life disciplined and live like a hermit - Discipline means monitoring oneself i.e., keeping a constant watch on one's own actions and conducts by obeying Yama, Niyama and good conducts. That is, following non-violence, truth and celibacy, keeping oneself away from lies, hypocrisy, useless conversation, addiction and keeping the mind engaged in God. Maintain purity of mind, tenacity, contentment and self-restrained.

3. Keep an eye on the movement of your mind - Whenever the mind becomes fickle, one should pay attention to one's incoming breath and should chant the name of God with each breath, without making sound.
4. Try to convert negative emotions of mind into positive through mediation or modification, peace and wisdom. Always engage the mind in good works and do not make raga (attachment) and malice (hatred) with any object, subject and person. Keep yourself away from Television news, political and crime newspapers because they are the transmitter of negative thoughts.
5. Engage the mind in the study and listening of the holy scriptures like Upanishads, Bhagavad Gita, Gurugranth Sahib, Dhammapada (Buddhist holy book), Tattvārthasūtra,(Jain holy book), Kabirvani and Patanjali Yoga Sutras. As the nutritious food is required to maintain good health, similarly, the healthy feeding of mind is required to have a clean, compose and stable mind.
6. Engage your mind in the regular practice of pranayama, meditation, Asana and devotion to Lord. Understand the value of this human life and do not waste it. The ultimate goal of human life is the attainment of Moksha, Nirvana or Kaivalya, that is, liberation from the cycle of birth and death. Keep the mind detached from negativity, drive the life away from ignorance.
7. Mind is the source of all evil. The mind of every person is his biggest enemy if it is left unbridled. The mind itself creates delusion and ignorance like a magician and activates the five thieves sitting inside a person and kills his wisdom. The five thieves i.e., sensuality, anger-hatred, greed, ego and attachment. With the help of these five thieves the mind keeps the man dancing. The only way out of the illusion of the mind is meditation, Vipassana.

We should learn to live like a lotus flower in this world. This world is full of all kinds of evils. Sometimes the darkness of ignorance is seen everywhere, but in that darkness too, we have to find the light inside ourselves by going inward. How does a lotus flower bloom in the midst of the mud? A lotus flower remains untouched by the impurity of the mud. Because of this, the lotus flower often represents purity of heart, body and mind which are also the three important elements of yoga.

In Buddhism, the lotus flower is a spiritual symbol of growth and enlightenment. Its colourful open petals get strength and support by the long-stalk inside the water which inspire its seed to bloom. Like a lotus flower, we can attain spiritual height and grow beautifully in the midst of bondage, maya and darkness all around.

FOURTH CHAPTER - SPIRITUAL STORIES

1
THE REALITY OF HUMAN LIFE

A man from a village was going to the city for some work. Although the city was not far away but the way to the city was difficult and deserted. The path passed through a dense forest. As the road was deserted, the man was walking fast towards the city. After going a little distance, he found some bones lying on the way, but he paid no attention to it and kept going forward. Then after walking some distance, he saw some more bones lying on the path, but he again did not pay any attention to it and kept moving forward. After walking a little farther, he again found some bones lying on the road and when he looked closely, he found that all the bones were of the human body. He thought that the wild animals in this dense forest must have eaten the passers-by. Meanwhile, he saw a lion standing far away on the road. After seeing the lion, the man became baffled. His suspicion now changed into belief that the lion must have eaten the passers-by. Now he started running backwards swiftly, to save his life. While running, he climbed on a banyan tree on the bank of a lake, but he became puzzled when he saw that the lion also followed him and climbed on the same tree. After seeing the lion, the man immediately grabbed the rope like long prop root hanging from that banyan tree. He thought that the lion would not be able to touch the rope. The banyan branch from which the man was hanging was spread towards the lake. When he looked down, he saw two huge crocodiles inside the lake which made him very scared. The situation of that man was very pathetic. On the one side the lion was sitting ready to eat him and on the other side two terrible crocodiles of the lake were ready to swallow him. He was very upset with this condition. In the meantime, he saw that the rope was being nibbled by two rats with their sharp teeth. Among those two mice, one was white and the other was black. Now the man was having trouble all around.

Meanwhile, the man saw honey dripping from a bee hive on the banyan tree. The man moved his mouth in front of the drops of honey and began to taste the honey. He forgot all his grief for a while and started enjoying it.

When Lord Buddha was narrating this story during his sermon, one of the crowd members spoke out loudly and said - Oh Buddha! How foolish was that man who despite of danger all around, forgot everything and started tasting the honey?

Then Lord Buddha smiled and said that the man was nobody else but you and all the people present here. Everybody was surprised by the words of Buddha. A man said, Oh Buddha! Kindly explain the meaning of this story. Then Lord Buddha said that the human bones lying on the path indicate that the people are dying every day. Go and see at the crematorium, how many people are dying every day. The lion symbolized the Yama (God of death) waiting for us to die. No one has any idea that when death will come. Two crocodiles are sexual desire and anger which are our hidden enemies ready to swallow us. Two mice, that is, white and black mice, are the symbol of day and night, which are shortening the rope of human life day by day, that is, man's age is getting reduced day by day. The drops of honey symbolized some of the physical and emotional pleasures in life.

Lord Buddha further said that human being is surrounded by sorrows from all sides still he is not conscious and repeatedly comes to this world to reap the fruits of his karma. In this way, the endless cycle of birth and death goes on. He does not make any effort to get out of this life cycle. If man tries, then nirvana (salvation) can be attained which will free him from the cycle of birth and death forever. Then sorrow will end forever. Lord Buddha advised the people to get out of ignorance and understand the reality of human life and try for nirvana.

2
AS YOU SOW, SO YOU REAP

It is an ancient story. In a village lived a very poor man. He was a labourer. He got grains as a wage in lieu of his work. In those days there was less practice of giving money. Price was determined by the grain.

He used to store the grains earned by his work inside an earthen container. He used to do hard labour to earn his wages. He used to bring grains every day, but still the quantity of grain was not increasing. He thought that someone was stealing his grains. In order to catch the thief, one day he was hiding in his hut and watched that a fat rat came and was eating his grains quickly. He understood that the fat rat has been eating his grains. The labourer ran to kill the rat, but that mouse did not run away. He spoke like a man and said – listen to me, dear brother, no matter how much labour you do, but you will not get more than this. It's your fate.

The labourer became very sad after hearing the rat's words. He started thinking that he will never get rid of his miserable life. Then the mouse said – 'Listen brother, don't get disappointed, you go to Lord Buddha. He is extremely knowledgeable. He knows everything. He will definitely tell you a solution that will change your fate.'

The labourer left his home in search of Lord Buddha with some food items for the way. He was tired after walking a long distance. It was going to be night. He thought that it would be appropriate to halt the journey till the morning. He saw a big house in front. That house belonged to a merchant. The labourer told the merchant that he wants to rest here overnight. Merchant asked him where he was going. Then the labourer said, 'I am going to meet Lord Buddha for a solution to get rid of the miseries of my life. People consider Lord Buddha an enlightened person and he will definitely show me some way.' Then the merchant said that his only daughter is dumb since her childhood. He showed her many doctors but no result came. He requested the labourer to do him a favour and ask Lord Buddha when his daughter will be able to speak.

In the morning the labourer set out on his journey. On the way he found a mountain. He climbed that mountain with great difficulty. He found a magician on the top of the mountain. The magician asked the labourer, where was he going all alone? Then the labourer said that he was going to meet Lord Buddha. He narrated everything to the magician. Then the magician said that – 'Brother, I am fed up with the life of this magician and want to get rid of it. Just ask Lord Buddha, when will I get rid of this magician's life.' The magician offered his magic baton to the labourer which took him across the mountain. At the bottom of the hill, he found a river in which water was flowing at a very high speed. The labourer thought that it would be difficult to cross this river. Suddenly he saw a very big tortoise. The tortoise asked the labourer – 'Oh brother! Where are you going through this deserted path?' Then the labourer said that he was going to ask Lord Buddha about remedy for his suffering. I have heard that there is an ashram near a forest at some distance from this mountain. Then the tortoise said – 'Do not worry about crossing the river. I will help you to cross the river. Please sit on my back. Kindly ask my one question to Lord Buddha. Right now, I am more than a hundred years old. Now I am bored with this life and I want to fly like a bird in the sky. My question is that when will I be able to fly in the sky as a bird?'

The labourer crossed the river and after traveling for a few hours, he reached the ashram of Lord Buddha. He saw that many people from far and wide had come to Lord Buddha with their questions. Meanwhile, a monk from the ashram of Lord Buddha urged people and said that one person can ask only three questions to Lord Buddha.

Seeing the crowd of people, such rules of the ashram have been made. Lord Buddha will not answer more than three questions.

The labourer thought that he has four questions, first his own question, second merchant's dumb daughter's question, the third the question of that of magician and the fourth, the question of that tortoise. The labourer was in a dilemma as to which question should be removed. He thought that the sorrow of the three of them is bigger than his. I am a daily wage earner, I am getting my meals without any difficulty, but what will happen to the daughter of the merchant who is dumb since childhood. It is a big question of the magician who has been waiting for liberation for years and that tortoise who is more than a hundred years old and is bored of his life. Thus, he should forget about his own question. He asked the other three questions to Lord Buddha. Then Lord Buddha said that -

1. The merchant's daughter will start speaking only when she would meet the life partner of her previous birth.
2. The magician will be free from this life only when he will abandon his magic baton.
3. The tortoise will become a bird when it will remove its shell.

The labourer bowed down before Lord Buddha and began to return home after getting answers of all his three questions. While returning, he first met the tortoise. The tortoise asked the answer to his question. Then the labourer told him that when it will remove its outer shell, only then it will be able to become a bird. The tortoise told the labourer that first you sit on my back and cross the river. The labourer crossed the river sitting on the back of the tortoise. Then the tortoise said to the labourer that 'now you remove my shell. On removing my shell, you will get many rare and precious pearls from my body. These pearls will give you enough money.' The labourer did the same and the tortoise turned into a beautiful bird and paid thanks to labourer and started flying freely in the sky.

The labourer while returning home met the magician on the hill.

The labourer told the magician that he will get freedom from his life only when he will give up his magic wand. The magician gave his magic wand to the labourer and said that this magic wand will remove your poverty.

The labourer proceeded for his home. On the way, he approached merchant's house and told the merchant that his only daughter will get cured when she would meet her previous birth life partner. As the labourer proceeded to return to his home by answering merchant's questions, merchant's dumb daughter saw the labourer from her balcony and she began to say loudly, "Father, to whom are you talking?" The merchant was surprised to hear the voice from his daughter's mouth for the first time and thought that the labourer was none other than the companion of his daughter's previous life. The merchant immediately stopped the labourer and said that now you marry my daughter and stay in this mansion of mine. You and my only daughter are the inheritors of my crores of property. The labourer got married to the merchant's daughter and his life changed drastically. He got a mansion, crores of property, magic baton, rare pearls and a gentle and noble wife. There was happiness in his life.

The meaning of this Buddhist story is that if a person who forgets his own sorrow and thinks about the good of other people and does good work, gets natural grace and the bad karma of his previous life is removed. Auspicious and happy changes start happening. That is why it is said that, do good to get good.

3
FRUIT OF PIOUS DEED AND DEVOTION

An ordinary farmer lived in a village. He had only one and half acres of land. That farmer was very hard working and farming was his life. He had two children in his family besides his wife. He loved his animals very much and took care of them as the member of his family.

The farmer used to put only manure prepared from cattle dung and leaves in his field and used to cultivate only vegetables. While other farmers of his village used to apply chemical fertilizer in their fields. He thought that it is wrong to cause harm to the health of other people for his own benefit. He was a devotee of Lord Shiva and thought that Lord Shiva would punish him for doing bad deed. Because of this, he was always conscious of his deeds. He was a clean man by mind and heart. That farmer used to provide food to saints and fakirs on the second day of Mahashivaratri every year. On Mahashivaratri the devotees of lord Shiva chant the name of Shiva whole night, while remaining in fasting. Apart from farming, he spent his time in devotion of Lord Shiva. People used to call him Shivadas.

A lot of vegetables were produced in every season due to the grace of lord shiva and the hard work of Shivdas. His farm vegetables were very tasty, so all vegetables were sold at his home. He did not have to go to the market to sell vegetables. People from far and wide used to come to buy vegetables.

Gradually Shivdas became a prosperous farmer. He bought three acres of land and also built a nice house. Many people of the village became jealous of his progress. A jealous man planned to steal in Shivdas's house. One day Shivdas went to a distant village to meet his married elder sister. Taking advantage of that opportunity, the jealous person sent two thieves to steal at Shivdas's house.

At around two o'clock in the night, when Shivdas's wife and children were in deep sleep, two thieves entered his house by putting a dent in the wall of his house. When the two thieves entered the house, both of them became like a blind man and were not able see anything except the trident of Lord Shiva. Both of them felt as if the trident would kill them. Both the thieves became frightened and ran away from the house in fear. That envious person of the village asked the thieves, why they were so scared? Then both the thieves said that Lord Shiva is guarding the Shivdas's house. Lord Shiva and his trident was ready to kill us. On hearing this, the jealous person became frightened and he stopped being envious to Shivdas.

In fact, the power of true karma and devotion is vast. God always helps a true devotee.

4
YOUR GOD IS INSIDE YOU

A rich farmer lived in a village. He was a very religious person. He used to go to the temple every day to worship God. He also got built many temples. He also travelled to many pilgrimage sites, yet he was unhappy due to the fact that even after doing so much efforts he could not see God.

Some villagers said to the farmer that only Buddha like seer can answer why till now you did not have a glimpse of God. Buddha has great inner sight and he knows everything. Why don't you go to Buddha to ask about this secret?

The next day the farmer went to Buddha's ashram and met him and told him everything. Then the Buddha said, come after two o'clock tomorrow to get the answer to your question.

That farmer was very keen to know the secret and was waiting eagerly for the time to come. On the second day just after two o'clock, he reached the ashram of Buddha. At that time Buddha was looking for something outside his ashram. Some other monks were also helping Buddha to find the object. When that farmer saw Buddha looking for something outside the ashram, he asked - oh Buddha! What are you looking for? Buddha said that one of his precious pearls has been lost. That farmer also started searching for that pearl. It was evening while searching. Now the farmer began to doubt on Buddha. He thought that how is he a great sage who doesn't even know about his lost pearl. Then how can he answer my question? Mahakashyapa, a senior monk of the ashram, was smiling while sitting at one place. Then another monk asked Mahakashyapa - Oh Mahakashyapa! Buddha is getting upset for the lost pearl and you are sitting and smiling. Mahakashyapa told the monk that nothing is unknown to Buddha, he is doing all this only to convince the farmer.

Getting upset while searching the pearl, the farmer asked Buddha, "Hey Buddha, please remember exactly where you kept the pearl." Perhaps you lost the pearl inside the ashram. Please search the pearl inside the Ashram. Now there is no sense searching it outside. Then Buddha said while explaining to the farmer that as the pearl is inside the ashram and there is no use searching it outside, similarly, your God is inside you and you have been searching him outside in temples and pilgrimages for so many years. Now the words of Buddha opened the eyes of the farmer. Farmer said - Oh great Buddha! Kindly help me to meet my God whom I am searching for a long time.

Buddha asked for a mat from a monk and told the farmer that now you sit on this mat in the posture of Padmasana. Close your eyes and forget the whole world for a while. Now you just concentrate on the anterior part of your nose and keep watching your incoming breaths from the inside vision. The farmer did the same by obeying Buddha. Gradually, his breathing started slowing down and his body sense also started disappearing and after a few hours he went into deep meditation.

Buddha told one of his monks that this farmer has now reached the stage of samadhi. The farmer remained in a state of samadhi for about five hours. When the samadhi was over, the farmer became very calm and happy. After some time, he got up from his seat and fell at the feet of Buddha and said that my life is successful today. He said, I saw my God. I wasted my valuable time in vain here and there. A guru like you has helped me to see my God inside me.

In the state of samadhi, there is a feeling of realisation of self and after that all the delusions of the person disappears. The experiences of the state of samadhi cannot be explained in words. One cannot understand the experience of ecstasy of samadhi without going through such experience. That experience is the experience of the ultimate truth which is indescribable.

Saint Kabir says –

'Jyon gunga ke sain ko gunga hi pahichan
Tyon gyani ke sukh Ko gyani habai so Jan.'

The signs of a dumb can be understood by a dumb only, similarly, the pleasure of divine- experience can be known by only a person who has got divine experience.

5
THINKING MAKES AND RUINS A MAN

Positive thoughts can elevate a man, while negative thoughts eventually lead him to ruin. A yogi sitting in a cave in the Himalayas allows his mind to wander for unwanted things, while a cobbler is engaged in repairing shoes at one corner of the crossroads of the city. The second is a better yogi than the first of these two.

A sanyasi lived in his ashram near a temple. A prostitute also lived nearby the ashram of sanyasi. Immoral and lascivious people used to come to the house of the prostitute. Once the sanyasi called the prostitute and warned her for her evil deeds. That day the prostitute expressed regret and prayed to the sanyasi for apology. However, she did not leave her profession due to compulsion.

The angry sanyasi started recording the immoral deeds and flaws of that prostitute and for this he started keeping a piece of stone for each of the evil deed in one corner of his ashram every day. When the pieces of stones became a heap, the sanyasi called the prostitute in the presence of the people and strongly condemned her. While denouncing her sins he showed the pile of stones as a pyramid of sins. That night the prostitute appealed to the Lord 'please end this sinful body of mine'. Incidentally the prostitute died that night due to heart attack. Surprisingly, the same night that sanyasi also passed away from this world. The prostitute's corpse was thrown as food to the vultures and carnivorous animals, but the sanyasi's last rites was performed with reverence. The sight of this event of the earth was completely different in Yamaloka. The prostitute's soul was sent to heaven, while the sanyasi's soul was sent to hell. Exasperated sanyasi's soul sought an explanation for this injustice. The reply was given that the mind of the sanyasi was always covered with unholy worries, while the prostitute was doing impious job by her body due to compulsion to earn her livelihood. Although her body was impure, but her mind was always engaged in the devotion of God. Both earthly remains were properly disposed off in the world, but their souls awarded according to their thinking. Therefore, always keep the mind pure.

6
PREGNANT DEER AND HUNTER

Once upon a time, a pregnant deer in a forest was suffering from labour pains. She was looking for a suitable place where she could give birth to her baby. After searching, she found a bush on the bank of a river which was safe from all four sides. The place was surrounded by the river on one side and the forest on the other.

When the female deer was about to give birth to her baby, suddenly she saw crisis from all sides. On one side a hunter was standing ready to hunt the deer and on the other side a lion was seen sitting in search of prey. The crisis deepened further when a fire broke out in the forest. The deer saw a disappointing situation from all sides. However, the deer also had no other option. She could not even run away at the time of childbirth. Eventually, the deer left her fate at the mercy of God. Deer now stopped thinking and gave birth to her baby safely.

In the meantime, a few incidents suddenly happened. The lightning struck in the sky and fell near the hunter and the hunter began to panic. He staggered, leaving the arrow from his hand, and the lion got injured with the arrow and it ran away.

The forest fire was extinguished due to heavy rains. Seeing this miracle, the deer thanked God. Now all her troubles were averted and everything was fine.

The lession from this story is that in adverse and difficult situation when one does not find any solution then everything should be left on the mercy of God, because everything happens due to the will of God.

7
TWO MONKS - A ZEN STORY

In the evening, two Buddhist monks were returning to their ashram. Just then there was heavy rain and the road was flooded with water. Both monks saw that a young woman wanted to cross the road but she was not able to cross the road due to excess water on the road. The senior of the two monks went to the young girl and ask her to sit on his back and he dropped her on the other side of the road. After that he went to the ashram with his companion.

In the evening the younger Buddhist monk went to the elder monk and said that – brother, being a monk, we cannot touch any woman. Yes - the elder monk replied. Again, the younger monk asked - but you had touched that young lady by carrying her on your back? Hearing this, the elder monk smiled and said - I had left her on the other side of the road, but you are still carrying her in your mind.

8
DIRTY CLOTHES - ZEN'S TALE

A Zen master lived in a village near the city of Osaka, Japan. He was famous and people from far and wide came to him to get their problems solved.

One day the Zen Master was on the morning walk with some of his disciples. On the way a rude man suddenly started hurling abusive language at Zen Master but the Zen Master did not react to his abusive words. Then the man also started abusing the Zen Master's parents, but the Zen Master kept calm and smiling. In the end, that rude man left that place. On the way the disciples asked the Zen Master - why did you not teach a lesson to that indecent man? If you had permitted us, we would have taught him a lesson. The Zen Master did not reply to the questions of his disciples. By then, Zen Master reached his home.

The Zen Master asked his disciples to wait at the door and in a few minutes, he brought out some smelly dirty clothes and gave them to his disciples. He said – 'take your clothes off and wear these clothes.'

Bad smell was coming from those clothes and the disciples threw them. Then Zen Master said - what happened? You cannot wear these clothes, right, then how could I accept the abuses thrown by that rude person? This is why I did not respond him. If you play with mud, mud will fall on you as well.

9
THE EFFECT OF SNAKE'S LENIENCY

Once a monk was passing through a village. The people of the village told the monk not to go through that path, because a poisonous snake lived in a hole under a mango tree. So far, that snake had bitten and killed many people.

The monk told the villagers that he knew the mantra, because of which that snake would not bite him. When the monk was passing through that path, the snake came out of its hole after hearing the man's footsteps and wanted to attack the monk. The monk hypnotized the snake with mantra and said, 'why are you biting the villagers and spoiling your karma?' To bite any person needlessly is wrong and a sin. The monk's persuasion had a great effect on the snake and it gave up its tendency to harm others and became completely calm.

When the villagers came to know that the snake is no longer biting anybody, some mischievous boys of the village started troubling the snake. An evil-natured boy grabbed the snake's tail and threw it away by rolling it round and round, due to which the snake was hurt and blood was coming from its mouth. The poor snake lay unconscious for a while and when it regained its consciousness, it slowly entered into its hole. Now it was very afraid of the human beings.

After a few days the monk was again passing through that village. The monk asked the villagers about the snake. The villagers said that the snake has now died. It has not been seen since several days. The monk himself went to the snake's hole to confirm this news and called it. The snake recognized the monk's voice and it came out moaning from its hole. The monk asked the snake who was responsible for its plight. Then the snake told that, 'obeying you, I had given up the path of violence. But the villagers, considering it my weakness, abused and injured me.'

The monk took out some ayurvadic medicines from his bag and rubbed some of them on the snake's body and fed some medicines to it and said that it would be well now. The monk loved the snake and told it that it is very difficult for anyone to know about the nature of human being by face, because nature varies from person to person. Some people are kind, gentle, righteous and generous while some are deceptive, wicked, merciless and sadistic. A person with low and unrighteous nature considers non-violence to be a weakness. Therefore, do not consider everyone equally. First try to understand the nature of man. If he is a good person, treat him with decency, but always be alert on seeing the wicked. Drive the wicked person away by 'hissing', don't do violence but don't give up your 'hiss.' This is wisdom. Every creature has the right of self-defence. God has also given weapons for self-defence to everyone. As God has given two hands and wisdom to human beings, he has given poison to you for the self-defence. You should not misuse the power given by God. But you may bite someone who wants to kill you. You too have right to live on this earth as human beings. God has created this earth for all beings. Saying this, the monk went ahead from there.

The snake became very happy with the knowledge given by the monk and started living its life according to the sermon of the monk.

10
STORY OF THREE HERMITS

The story of 'Three Hermits' is written by the famous Russian writer Leo Tolstoy. The famous books of Leo Tolstoy are 'War and Peace' and 'The Kingdom of God is Within You.'

Once a bishop was traveling by ship to the Solovetsky monastery located on the Solovetsky Islands in the White Sea in northern Russia. During the voyage, some fishermen told the bishop that there are three monks living on the same island who are known for their simplicity, honesty, purity and happy mind. The mind becomes pure and blissful by seeing those three ascetics. Some fishermen also told that once their boat got stuck in mud then all the three hermits helped to get it out.

After hearing about the three ascetics, the bishop was curious to meet these ascetics. The bishop wanted to know how the three hermits worshiped God.

After completing the journey, the bishop got off his ship and reached Solovetsky Monastery first, disposed off all his works there and reached the hut of the three ascetics located on the same island on the second day. The bishop sought to know from those three ascetics how they worshiped God. Those three ascetics told the bishop that they always say – 'Oh God! You are our dearest. You're very kind. You always have mercy on us.' Hearing this prayer method of the ascetics, the bishop found it very simple and he suggested the method of worshiping God by singing certain verses of the Bible.

On the same night, the bishop was to return from there by the ship. In the moonlit night, the ship started moving in the ocean. The bishop did not sleep in the ship and began to watch the sea from the ship. After a while, the bishop saw three moon-like figures floating on the sea. All the three luminous images were approaching the ship. The ship pilot also watched with curiosity those three men like figures coming towards the ship by floating on the sea. The bishop and the ship's pilot were very surprised to see that the same three hermits were coming near the ship. All three of them sitting on the sea told the bishop that they had forgotten some lines of the verse which the bishop had told them. They asked, 'Oh Bishop! Please recite it again.'

The bishop was surprised to see the innocence, humility, simplicity and miracle of the three ascetics and told them that the method by which you are worshiping God is the best. My ignorance has been removed by just your glimpse. I have nothing to teach you, but I have much to learn from you. The bishop greeted all three ascetics with folded hands. The bishop's ship went ahead and the three monks returned to their huts.

11
VALUE OF LIFE

Once a man from a village came to the ashram of Lord Buddha and asked him – 'Oh Buddha! What is the value of this life?' Hearing that villager, Lord Buddha smiled and gave him a shining stone and said that after knowing the value of this shining stone you may be able to know the answer of your question. But remember that you do not have to sell this stone, but you have only to find out the price of this stone and come back. First of all, the villager showed that stone to a vegetable vendor and asked the price of the stone. The vegetable seller told him, 'Although the stone is of no use to me, but it is beautiful to see, so you take any vegetable you want in lieu of this stone and give this stone to me.'

Then the villager took that stone and showed it to a fruit seller and asked for its price. The fruit seller said, 'this stone looks very beautiful and it can be used in the decoration of my shop. You take five dozen fruits in exchange for this stone and give it to me.'

The villager again showed the stone to a goldsmith. The goldsmith said, 'it is some precious stone. You take one lakh silver coins and give it to me.'

Finally, the villager went to a jeweller who only traded in diamonds and jewels. The jeweller looked at the stone very carefully and said, 'it is a rare diamond. You take my all property in exchange for this stone and give it to me.' Hearing the jeweller's words, the villager was stunned and came back to Lord Buddha and said everything to him. Then Lord Buddha told the villager that this life is priceless. The other people estimate your value or evaluate your life according to their thinking and understanding. Every person's understanding and assessment is different, as the vegetable vendor, fruit seller, goldsmith and the jeweller valued the price of the same item differently according to their understanding and assessment. The jeweller valued right price of the stone, because the jeweller has the understanding to recognize precious stones. Thus, your life is also precious. Only a jeweller can understand you. Be a jeweller of your life and recognize the potential inside you and do not waste your life in vain.

12
EVERYTHING IS IMPERMANENT IN THIS WORLD

It was eight o'clock in the night. A Zen Mahatma was entering the palace of the king. The guard did not stop him from going inside. He knew Zen Mahatma. At that time, the king was walking in the verandas of his palace. The king saw the Mahatma. The king asked the Zen Mahatma 'what is the reason for your coming to the royal court at this time?' Mahatma said, 'I have to take my night's rest in this inn.' The king said to Mahatma – 'this is a palace, not an inn.' The Mahatma replied - This may be a palace for you but for me it is just an inn. The king expressed his displeasure over this remark of the Mahatma. Then the Mahatma asked the king who got this palace built? Then the king replied that this palace was got built by his great grandfather. Then the Zen Mahatma said that your great-grandfather lived in this palace, but he left this palace long before. Then your grandfather and father lived in this palace. They too left this palace. Now you live in this palace. After some time, you too will leave this palace. In this way, new people keep coming to this palace and old people leave this palace. Thus, the process of coming and going in this palace continues. Men keep coming and going in the inn too. Be it the palace or the inn or the world, the process of coming and going continues. People who come to this world ignorantly remain fascinated with palaces, houses, land and property, whereas all things are temporary. Oh king! This body of yours is also temporary. This world is temporary like an inn. There is an endless cycle of going and coming here. Therefore, you, please come out of your ignorance.

Mahatma's words brought awakening in the king and he thought that Mahatma was right. In this world, everything is impermanent.

13
RESULT OF NEGATIVE AND POSITIVE THOUGHTS

Once in Vaishali (a place in Bihar near Patna), Lord Buddha was telling the monks that the thoughts of mind play an important role in life. The thought of the mind can have good or bad results. The thought of mind can make a man a deity or a demon. Lord Buddha told a story.

Once the king of Udantpur was passing through the city road by his chariot. When the king passed through a sandalwood shop, his mind got very irritated on seeing the sandalwood shopkeeper. He thought that this shopkeeper should either be killed by sword or crushed to death by an elephant.

When the king returned from the city and came to his palace, he started cogitating over the incident and thought why he had negative thoughts after seeing the sandal wood shopkeeper. The king summoned the wise minister to his palace and asked the minister why did negative thoughts developed after seeing the sandal wood shopkeeper? The minister was wise. He told the king that he needed a few days to answer this. The king gave the minister one week's time.

After a day, the minister changed his attire and went like a common man to that sandal wood merchant and sat near him and asked him about the condition of his business. The businessman said that the business is going very bad. He said many people come to my shop and see the sandal wood, sniff it and also praise the sandal wood, but no man buys even a piece of sandalwood. My business has collapsed.

I am thinking that the king of this kingdom may die so that all my sandalwood sticks could be sold for his funeral.

Now the minister understood that due to the negative thoughts of this businessman, negative sentiment had arisen in the mind of the king. After knowing this, the minister went to his house. On the next day he sent a man to buy a small bundle of sandal wood from the shop of sandalwood merchant. He presented that bundle to the king saying that this sandal wood's bundle has been sent by sandalwood shopkeeper as a gift for him. The king, after accepting that gift, smelled those sandalwood sticks and was very pleased with the scent. The king thought that the sandalwood shopkeeper is a nice person and then why did he have negative feeling against him? The king, regretting his mistake, ordered one of his orderly to give some gold coins on his behalf to the merchant of sandalwood and in addition to that he told him to purchase some more bundles of sandalwood from his shop.

The king's orderly gave some gold coins as a gift from the king to the sandal wood shopkeeper as per the king's order and also gave him a lot of gold coins and bought the remaining sandal wood. The sandalwood shopkeeper now started thinking that his king is a nice person but why did he have negative feelings against him.

After narrating this story, Lord Buddha said that as we sow so we reap. If we have a positive attitude towards other, then that will generate positive feelings and if there is a negative emotion then it will create a negative emotion. Therefore, renouncing negative emotions is very important for self-happiness.

14
BOTH HAPPINESS AND SORROW ARE TEMPORARY

Once a king asked the scholars and theologists present in his court that they should tell him a formula which is valuable for life. Everybody started thinking about the valuable formula. Then an elderly scholar told the king that there is a hut of a saint near the forest outside the city. Only he can answer this question. The king went to the saint and touched his feet and then put his question before him. The saint said that while giving me a talisman my Guru had said that whenever you get stuck in a difficult situation and find no solution to it, then open this talisman which has a valuable formula. This will guide you in the critical time in life. The saint told the king that no such awful situation has yet come in my life and I am a saint, I don't need it. You are a king you need this talisman more than me. Take this talisman, but remember that it has to be opened only in time of calamity. The king returned to his palace with the talisman given to him by the saint and tied the talisman in his arm.

Everything was going well in the king's life, but after some time the neighbouring enemy king invaded his kingdom and defeated him in the battle. After being defeated, the king was running away to save his life from the enemy's army and the enemy's army was chasing him. In this bad time, many soldiers and officers of his kingdom changed their loyalties and joined the conquering king. At this bad time only his horse and a few loyal soldiers were with the king. The king was saving his life by hiding here and there. One day the king was disappointed while sitting hiding in a mountain cave, then he suddenly remembered the talisman given to him by the saint. He remembered that the saint had said to open this talisman in bad time. The king thought that the time has come to open this talisman. When the king opened the talisman tied in his arm, it had a couplet- 'This time will also go'. After reading this sutra, the king's mind got satisfied. He started living comfortably in the cave of that mountain and gradually started increasing his strength. After some time, some people rebelled against the enemy king inside the kingdom. Taking advantage of this time, the king attacked to reclaim his kingdom and regained his kingdom by killing the king of the enemy kingdom.

To celebrate the victory, a very big event took place in the king's court, in which dance and songs were going on. All the people were very happy and were enjoying the event, but the king remembered the couplet of that talisman again and again - 'This time will also go'. The king now understood that both happiness and sorrow are temporary. This is the reason why the wise people always live in detachment, that is, in equanimity. Both suffering and happiness are temporary.

15
SAINT THIRUVALLUVAR

There are many similarities in the life of the great saint Thiruvalluvar of South India and saint Kabir, the great saint of North India. Both saints were weavers by profession and were fostered by another couple. The events of their childhood are similar as both were abandoned by the parents who gave them birth. Perhaps God has some desire behind such incidents because by taking inspiration from the lives of such great saints, the commoner can also achieve the highest level in their life. Both Saint Kabir and Saint Thiruvalluvar were like deities. Their contributions, words and vision will always illuminate and inspire the entire human beings. They tried their best to remove delusion of the people through their poems and teachings.

Like Saint Kabir, Saint Thiruvalluvar was a great poet without any formal education. Saint Kabir was a renowned Hindi poet whereas Thiruvalluvar was a famous Tamil poet. Thiruvalluvar's poems compositions are divided into three parts- Aram- (Virtues), Porul- (Government and Society) and Kamam- (Love). Both Saint Kabir and Saint Thiruvalluvar vehemently opposed casteism and hypocrisy. It is because of the high spiritual views of Saint Thiruvalluvar that Buddhists, Jains, Shaivites and Vaishnava claim that he was follower of their faith, whereas Saint Thiruvalluvar was above any caste and creed.

Actually, there is nothing definite about the date of birth, place of birth and family of Thiruvalluvar. It is believed that Thiruvalluvar lived in the city of Madurai and later Mayilapuram or Tirumalai (present-day Mylapore in Chennai). Some people say that he was born in Mayilapuram in the third century and later he moved to Madurai. Thiruvalluvar used to say that a man can lead a high spiritual life even in the domestic life. He told the people that there is no need to leave home to become sanyasi. His teachings now exist in the form of a book known as 'Tirukkural'.

The Thiruvalluvar statue, 133 feet height, has been erected on top of a rock in the ocean near the coast of Kanyakumari at the south of India's border near the confluence of the Arabian Sea, the Bay of Bengal and the Indian Ocean.

16
SAINT MILAREPA

In the spiritual history of Tibet, the place of Saint Milarepa is on the top after Lord Buddha. Saint Milarepa not only succeeded in eliminating the evil deeds of his life through his difficult spiritual practice, but by dint of his spiritual practice he attained enlightenment and nirvana. Milarepa is considered a great saint and a spiritual poet.

Milarepa was born in the province of Guangcheng in western Tibet, close to Nepal in the eleventh century. His teenage years went through a lot of difficulties. Although he was born into a prosperous family but his father died when he was just seven years old. His uncle was responsible for the maintenance of his mother and sister besides Milarepa, but instead of caring for them, his uncle took all his property and started mistreating his family. Thus, the life of Milarepa's family became very painful. Despite several attempts, his uncle flatly refused to give the property of Milarepa's father. That made Milarepa's mother feel very angry. When Milarepa was thirteen years old, his mother instigated Milarepa to take avenge for his uncle's injustice and sent him to a tantric to learn tantra to destroy his uncle.

Many years passed in learning tantra. Meanwhile his mother and sister died due to poverty and disease. When Milarepa returned his home after learning tantra, he came to know that his mother and sister were no longer in this world. Knowing this, Milarepa got a feeling of vengeance for his uncle and in the meantime, he got an opportunity to carry out this vengeance. When his uncle's son was to get married, at that time, Milarepa made fierce hail rain by the power of his tantra knowledge, which led to the death of many family members along with his uncle and aunt.

In this way, Milarepa took his revenge. But due to this vengeance, his mind became restless. He started thinking that he had taken lives of many people for vengeance. When he told his tantric guru about the restlessness of his mind, the tantric guru said that he had misused the power of tantra. Its fruit will not be good. It is not appropriate to misuse any knowledge.

The tantric guru suggested him that by following the path of meditation practice he could get rid of the bad karma. He further advised Milarepa to go to meditation and spiritual master Marpa. Marpa was a disciple of the famous spiritual guru Naropa and who had considerable fame in that area.

Milarepa went out to meet the spiritual master Marpa and reached his village. At that time Marpa was ploughing his field. After knowing the story of Milarepa, Marpa did not show any sympathy to him, on the contrary he refused to give him knowledge and mistreated him. Milarepa built several houses for Marpa by his hard labour but Marpa demolished those houses. Milarepa was doing work like a servant by obeying his Guru in the hope that one day his guru would give him knowledge. Milarepa spent almost a decade in the hope of knowledge from Marpa and eventually he got frustrated. One day he decided to put an end to his life and went to a secluded place to commit suicide. At that point, he was called by Guru Marpa who embraced Milarepa and said that now you have become worthy of getting knowledge. Guru Marpa told Milarepa that he wanted to cleanse his mind from his bad deeds by giving him troubles that is why he had to go through a tough test. But due to patience and self-confidence, he faced all the difficult situations with courage.

Guru Marpa began to impart spiritual knowledge to Milarepa and in the end he locked Milarepa in a cave to experience actual knowledge on his own. The cave was very narrow in which the light could hardly enter. Only the air could come for breath. After remaining in meditation for three days and three nights, he got some wonderful experience. To tell this experience to his guru he came out of the cave and wanted to know the meaning of it but Guru Marpa did not know anything about it. Milarepa again went to the cave to meditate. In the meantime Marpa went to know about this experience of Milarepa from his mentor Naropa. Then Guru Naropa told Marpa that this is an extraordinary experience and that the person who has got this experience can now attain Nirvana quickly by reaching at the spiritual height. Hearing this, Marpa was very surprised and started thinking that his disciple has now become his mentor and later Marpa became a disciple of Milarepa.

Milarepa had now touched the heights by intense meditation. His life changed completely due to the practice of continuous meditation. Later on, he became a great saint, hermit and an eminent spiritual poet. The life of Saint Milarepa is a source of inspiration for everyone. His life shows that if a person is determined then he can transform his life completely.

17 STORY OF SIDDHA YOGI BODHIDHARMA

Buddhism was propagated from time to time in China, Japan and Korea by Buddhist monks and saints of India. Today, the people of China, Japan and Korea are at the forefront in martial arts in the world. But very few people know about the progenitor of Martial arts in China. Perhaps people even do not know who had laid the foundation of the Zen sect of Mahayana Buddhism.

The foundation of Zen Buddhism and martial arts was laid down in China by Bodhidharma, who was a south Indian by birth. Bodhidharma's real name was Dharma Varma who was a prince of the Pallava dynasty in south India and was born in the fifth century. The rule of the Pallava dynasty extended to present-day Tamil Nadu, Andhra Pradesh and Karnataka. Its capital was Kanchipuram. In the same Pallava dynasty, Dharma Varma was born as the third son of King Narasimha Varma II, who later became Bodhidharma. His two elder brothers were Nandi Varma and Shiva Varma.

Bodhidharma had trouble of breathing in his childhood. For this reason, he was taught many types of pranayama, asana and meditation by the yoga gurus since the age of five, so that his breathing problem could be cured. Bodhidharma was very weak in his childhood, due to which he was made to practice many types of wrestling. His master ordered him to strengthen himself by moulding the body and mind as one unit and gradually he not only overcame his respiratory illness and physical weakness but he became champion of martial arts after four to five years of yoga practice. He defeated everyone in wrestling in his kingdom.

All religions were equally respected under the rule of the Pallava dynasty. There were many Buddhist monasteries in that state. The yoga guru of Bodhidharma was a Buddhist. His name was Prajnatara. The Buddhist yoga guru told Bodhidharma to always remember that man's greatest enemy is his mind. One who has controlled his mind can perform difficult tasks comfortably. Bodhidharma was greatly influenced by his Buddhist guru, therefore, he not only embraced Buddhism but he became a Buddhist monk, renouncing the splendour and pleasure of his kingdom to propagate Buddhism.

Bodhidharma is said to have not only mastered yoga, but he also studied the texts of Ayurveda such as Charaka, Sushruta, Dhanvantari, and gained a thorough knowledge about the roots of herbs and plants and their medicinal uses.

He left India at the age of twenty-eight and moved to China to spread the teachings of Buddhism. He lived in a cave near the Shaolin Temple in China. He practiced Zen meditation in China for a long time. He taught martial arts to the Chinese Buddhist monks of the Shaolin Temple and protected the people from the local bandits.

Once the King of Liang Dynasty of China came to meet Bodhidharma after hearing his fame. The King started praising him a lot, but Bodhidharma paid no attention to his praise. 'Tell me clearly for what reason you have come to me?' asked Bodhidharma to the king. The king said – 'Oh seer! I do not sleep properly and my mind keeps troubling me a lot.' Bodhidharma replied that there is bound to be disturbance in the life of a king. If you leave the crown, all your troubles will go away. On hearing Bodhidharma's words, the king felt that this man is talking like an insane, but the king wanted the remedy of his problem from Bodhidharma. Bodhidharma told the king, 'Come alone tomorrow morning and do not bring royal convoy with you and also bring your mind which is troubling you'. The king returned to his palace and at night he began to think that the monk is a strange person. After all, how can anyone catch one's mind? In the next morning the king went alone to meet Bodhidharma. Bodhidharma told the king, 'Sit on the ground and while sitting on the ground, you forget your kingdom and the world and keep watching your incoming breath with closed eyes.' The king followed Bodhidharma's order. Gradually the king's mind started cooling down. Bodhidharma called the king every day for the practice of meditation. Finally, the king got rid of his mental troubles. The king became the disciple of Bodhidharma and he got many meditation centres set up all over the country. It is said that Bodhidharma meditated inside a cave for many years and he became the greatest master of meditation after Lord Buddha. He spread the knowledge of meditation, yoga, martial arts and Ayurveda in China. Bodhidharma himself attained enlightenment and guided many people to attain enlightenment. The people of Japan call him Duruma.

Bodhidharma used to say that we search Buddha outside. This is our delusion. Buddha is there in every person. He advised the people to make mind free from negativity, i.e., ignorance and worldly craving. Bodhidharma used to say that 'people of deep understanding see within themselves and do not get deviated even a bit from the external environment.' Bodhidharma used to say that ignorance cannot be overcome without constant practice of meditation. Only after taming of mind and senses a man can be able to know his true nature.

18
REALISATION OF GOD

This is an old story. A Siddha yogi lived in a deserted place of a forest. He was always in penance. He had many Siddhis(para normal power) and divine knowledge. His aura was divine and after seeing him one got peace and bliss. When the ferocious animals of the forest came near him, they became calm and non-violent. Due to his divine force, the surrounding environment was purified. Due to this, both tigers and goats were living together.

A woodcutter used to go to the same forest every day to bring the dry woods. He used to see the Yogi. One day he thought that by selling dry wood in the market he is not able to support his family properly, so he should ask some remedy from the Yogi for his wellbeing. The woodcutter went near Yogi and offered obeisance to him and narrated his grief to him. Then the yogi out of compassion told him about a small hill near the forest and said that when you dig in the south direction of that hill, you will get gold which will remove your poverty but after that do not increase your greed. The woodcutter dug in the south direction of the hill according to Yogi's statement and he obtained a small bundle of gold and went home. Now that woodcutter started selling some of that gold. He started another business and gradually, he became a rich businessman. Now almost all the material comforts of life were available to him.

One day he was very peaceful and he thought that his poverty was removed by yogi. When the yogi was knowing about that gold, yet yogi had no attachment for the gold. This means that the yogi has got something more precious than the gold. He began to think over it.

One day the man went back to the forest again and bowed down to the yogi and asked, "Oh seer! I want to know from you, what wealth you have received which is more valuable than the gold." Yogi looking at the person's pure mind and innocence, told him that he knew about the gold and diamonds in this forest and the nearby hills through his divine eyes, but those gold and diamonds were of no use to him. These gold and diamonds create greed, attachment and lust that take us away from God. These worldly things cannot attract a person who has once experienced the God.

Then that person asked the yogi – 'Oh, seer! You have experienced that God, then how is that God?' Yogi said – God is neither male nor female. He is formless, unborn, all-pervading, compassionate, source of happiness and the root of everything in this world. The nature and all beings are born from Him and dissolve into Him. But the people are not able to see this God, because their mind is full of craving and craving is a veil of ignorance. You too can see that God like me, but to get that God you have to discard your worldly attachment. The mind has to be purified through detachment. After that, regular practice of meditation has to be done. Gradually, you have to get out of the trap of Maya (delusion) created by the senses and the mind and then you will be able to experience that God in the state of deep meditation, i.e., Samadhi. Once you see that God, then you will find that all the wealth and sensual happiness are useless. Once you know that ultimate truth, all your ignorance and confusion will be removed permanently.

The person started the practice of meditation to experience the God on the basis of the teaching given by the seer and eventually he realized the God.

RADHA KRISHNA KUMAR
(M.A. LL.B.)
Advocate
SUPREME COURT OF INDIA
email: radhakrishna.kumar@yahoo.com
WhatsApp number – 8447095995

A person knows many things about this world, but he is ignorant about himself. He doesn't know his true nature. Is man just a body made of the five elements, mind, the five sense organs, the five karma organs, or is he a form of Brahman? The Brihadaranyaka Upanishad says that 'Aham Brahmasmi' which means I am Brahman. The Chandogya Upanishad says that 'Tat tvam Asi', 'Tatvamasi' means that Brahman is in you, in me and in all living beings. The Aitareya Upanishad says - 'Pragyan Brahman', that is, the realization of Brahman is the true knowledge. However, a man can realize his Brahman form only in the state of Samadhi.

The man himself is the form of Brahman, but he does not realize it at all. He leaves this world by wasting life in ignorance. The teaching of Upanishads, the teaching of Samkhya (Jnana), Bhakti and Karma Yoga given by Lord Shri Krishna to Arjuna in Bhagavad Gita, the teachings of Lord Buddha, the teaching of Yoga Sutras of Maharishi

Patanjali and the verses of Saint Kabir helps us to come out of ignorance and lead us towards the true knowledge. All these teachings of sacred texts and great seers remind us repeatedly about our true nature and advise us to come out of the delusion.

Today, due to religious and sectarian narrowness man is becoming the enemy of his own mankind. Saint Kabir says - 'Hindu kahe Mohi Ram Pyara, Turk (Muslim) kahe Rahmana, wapas me dou ladi ladi muye, Maram Na Kou Jana.' Saint Kabir says that The Hindus and Muslims often fight due to communal misunderstanding. The common people are not aware of the true essence of religion. Today there is jealousy, hatred, discontent, anger and negative thoughts everywhere. Day by day humanity and human sensibility is vanishing, which is a threat to human existence. Love, fraternity, happiness, non-violence and compassion are the basis for making human life meaningful, which can be created only through spirituality and yoga.

The author through this book has tried to present the essence of religion, yoga and spirituality on the basis of the sacred scriptures, authentic texts and the thoughts of sages, so that the darkness of confusion and ignorance can be removed from human mind and positive thoughts may be generated in the world. In this book the characteristics of Dharma, God, soul, maya (delusion), avidya (ignorance), law of karma and the principle of reincarnation have been discussed. All religions, spirituality and yoga have been explained in detail so that this book can be useful for every human being.

www.ingramcontent.com/pod-product-compliance
Ingram Content Group UK Ltd.
Pitfield, Milton Keynes, MK11 3LW, UK
UKHW041827200726
13854UKWH00002BA/630

9 789395 217231